TABLE OF CONTENTS

The Stars Are Right

We just had a half-hour conversation here in the editorial pit at Paizo about what robots are called in Golarion. This is my job. I get paid to figure out what to call robots in a world where those menaced by violent metal men might not have come up with a word like "robot." And of course, we got distracted along the way by the Gearsmen of Numeria and me talking in a silly "Conan voice" and androids and all sorts of stuff that wasn't really addressing the question at hand. I think the whole situation, which dragged out for almost 30 minutes, may have cost Wes a few years of his life from the stress.

The best part is, you won't even find robots in this volume's adventure! That's not to say that there aren't strong science fiction elements awaiting you, though. "Children of the Void" is easily the most sci-fi we've gotten yet with a *Pathfinder* adventure, with its falling stars and strange aliens and the like. The inspiration for this adventure is firmly rooted in movies like *Night of the Creeps, Aliens, Invasion of the Body Snatchers, Day of the Triffids*... the list goes on and on. But at the same time, it's very much still a fantasy adventure. Sure, one of the main antagonists in the adventure rode down to Golarion on the back of a meteorite, but the akatas fit right in with any of the other strange creatures you see lurking in the depths of the game. I mean, would any self-respecting astroman blink twice after he steps out of his rocketship onto the surface of an alien planet only to be greeted by aliens that look like rust monsters, gibbering mouthers, or xills? You gotta be ready for the strangely shaped monsters if you're exploring deep space, and the game itself has no shortage of weirdos.

What I'm saying is that science fiction stories have a much stronger influence on the game that one might initially suspect. One of the game's classic adventures, *Expedition to the Barrier Peaks,* is the obvious example,

Pathfinder

Second Darkness

Children of the Void

CREDITS

Editor-in-Chief • James Jacobs
Art Director • Sarah E. Robinson
Managing Editor • F. Wesley Schneider
Editor • James L. Sutter
Copy Editor • Christopher Carey
Editorial Assistance • Jason Bulmahn,
Sean K Reynolds, and Vic Wertz
Editorial Intern • Claudia Golden
Graphic Design Assistance • Drew Pocza
Managing Art Director • James Davis
Publisher • Erik Mona

Cover Artist
Steve Prescott

Cartographer
Rob Lazzaretti

Contributing Artists
Concept Art House, Andrew Hou,
Ben Wootten, Kevin Yan, Iker Serdar Yildiz

Contributing Authors
Ashavan Doyon, Mike McArtor, Rob McCreary, Erik Mona, Ryan Z. Nock,
Sean K Reynolds, Amber Scott, James L. Sutter

Paizo CEO • Lisa Stevens
Vice President of Operations • Jeff Alvarez
Director of Marketing • Joshua J. Frost
Corporate Accountant • Dave Erickson
Staff Accountant • Christopher Self
Technical Director • Vic Wertz
Online Retail Coordinator • Jacob Burgess

Special Thanks
The Paizo Customer Service and Warehouse Teams

Paizo Publishing, LLC
2700 Richards Road, Suite 201
Bellevue, WA 98005
paizo.com

but there are plenty of others. Science fiction stories are a great place to search for monster ideas, which was the approach we took for this volume's Bestiary. You'll see man-eating plants (inspired by John Wyndham's classic *Day of the Triffids*), four-armed alien merchants (inspired by sword and planet stories like those of Edgar Rice Burroughs's Barsoom), and swarming beasts who use the bodies of their victims as incubators (inspired, of course, by the titular menace of *Alien*). Although the next four adventures in the Second Darkness Adventure Path don't drift as far into science fiction as this one does, you can expect to see some more aliens popping into the Bestiary now and then... including one that'll probably be *very* familiar to old-time players of the game!

Our science-fiction elements go beyond the adventure and the bestiary in this volume, in fact. On page 56, you'll find a gazetteer for the entire solar system! Golarion's just one of 11 planets orbiting the sun, and each of those other 10 planets is full of opportunities for adventure. We've tried to capture a different theme for each of them, but you certainly can't cover everything with less than a dozen planets. Fortunately for those who want Dyson spheres, binary stars, living planets, space stations, or even our Earth to join the campaign, you have a lot of room to add them in. The basic assumption is that the universe that Golarion occupies and the universe we occupy are, in fact, the same. It's a big enough place for pretty much any adventure you'd ever want to run.

And for the record, I think that we're gonna go ahead and just call them robots.

MCARTOR'S ALIENS

When we first started plotting out the Second Darkness Adventure Path, we were in a weird sort of limbo. We knew that a new edition of the game was going to be available at the same time the first of these adventures came out, but we didn't know if we would be using those rules, sticking with the 3.5 OGL, or what. This put me in a pretty awkward spot, since in order to assign an adventure, I have to be assured that writer will be familiar with the rules the adventure uses. Since I couldn't guarantee that a freelancer would be comfortable (or interested in) designing for new rules, should we go that route, I assigned the first four adventures of Second Darkness to editors here at Paizo. (Originally, I was going to write "Shadow in the Sky" myself, but fortunately Greg Vaughan was able to save my sanity and step in at the last minute to tackle that job!)

When I asked Mike McArtor if he wanted to write one of these adventures, his reaction was a combination of excitement and horror. He explained to me that he did indeed want to write one of the adventures, but was concerned because he'd never written one this long before. I pointed out to him that he had written plenty for several

of his other freelance projects (such as his last two works, *Guide to Korvosa* and *Guide to Darkmoon Vale*). Fortunately for me, that did the trick.

Of course, writing an adventure is actually quite a bit different than writing a sourcebook. In my own experience, writing adventures is a lot harder. You don't get the luxury of long stretches of flavor writing in an adventure (those pesky rules keep butting in), and worse, you can't just settle into one groove in one subsystem of rules. When you're writing an adventure, you get to jump back and forth from stat blocks to skill checks to new magic items to environmental hazards to pretty much anything else the story you're working on might call for. It ain't easy, in other words.

But Mike came through. He infused "Children of the Void" with just the right kind of sci-fi elements I was looking for—creepy aliens that arrive on a meteor, undead created by a more sci-fi genesis than one that's magical, and the undercurrent of people harvesting and using alien life forms as weapons against their own enemies. All popular themes in science fiction, and as you'll see in this adventure, quite potent themes for RPGs as well.

SORRY, STEVE!

So we messed up good on the credits page of *Pathfinder* #13. The cover artist for both the standard version (the one with the drow and the wererats) and the limited edition Gen Con alternate cover (the one with the elven general and the Riddleport scene depicting the falling star) were actually painted by Steve Prescott. (Wayne Reynolds is moving on to provide covers for several of our Pathfinder Chronicles books, for those wondering where he went.)

In fact, Steve Prescott's doing the covers for all of the Second Darkness volumes of *Pathfinder*. At the time I'm writing this foreword, we've seen four of the seven covers he'll be creating for us, and they're jaw-droppingly awesome—drow have never looked so cool!

We've got Steve properly credited on the credits page of this *Pathfinder* (let me go double check... yeah, there he is), but again, I'd like to apologize for the error in the credits for the previous volume. We love you, Steve!

James Jacobs
Editor-in-Chief
james.jacobs@paizo.com

Second Darkness
CHAPTER ✴ TWO

Children of the Void

In the passage of a heartbeat, the tiny island of Devil's Elbow changed forever. Known locally as the site of a failed settlement called Witchlight, and reputed to be haunted by the ghost of a notorious siren named Virashi, Devil's Elbow is destined to become known as the island where a star fell, and the site of a frenzied rush to claim the valuable skymetal the fallen star brought to Golarion. Yet the prospectors who arrive on Devil's Elbow are fated to find more than riches on the deadly island.

ADVENTURE BACKGROUND

Devil's Elbow is a mountainous island, heavily forested with pine trees, firs, redwoods, and cypress trees. Reefs and dangerous rocks surround the island except for one narrow approach to a sheltered cove on its northern side, and most of the island's shores are rocky cliffs averaging 100 feet in height. The island terrain itself is rugged, with its highest peak being 800 feet above sea level. Birds, bats, and other flying animals are common fauna, and there's a relatively large population of deer, wild boar, wild dogs, stirges, giant centipedes, snakes, donkey rats, and rabbits on the island as well. Most of these animals and vermin were introduced to the island by settlers from the south 5 decades ago.

At that time, Devil's Elbow was known primarily among the local Varisians and goblin tribes of the nearby mountains as the lair of a cruel and capricious siren named Virashi. When disenfranchised explorers and settlers began drifting into the region in great numbers 70 or so years ago, dissatisfied with the way Magnimar was growing, several settlements sprang up along the shores here. While two of these settlements (Riddleport and Roderic's Cove) fared well and even flourished, most of the settlements, faced with goblins, dangerous wildlife, and the difficulties of the remote region, did not. The village of Witchlight, founded in 4680 AR by an exiled Chelish merchant named Yaris Neraken, was one such village.

When he was scouting locations for a suitable site, he and his ship wrecked on the reefs surrounding Devil's Elbow. Yaris, the only survivor of the wreck, found himself in the care of a strange and enthralling creature with the body of a bird and the face of a beautiful woman—the siren Virashi. He spent many months as her plaything, but in time an amazing thing happened. The two fell in love. Virashi released Yaris from enthrallment, and while he remained at the siren's side for many more weeks, he pined for the comforts of civilization. He eventually convinced Virashi that, were he to establish a thriving community on the island above, not only would he be able to enjoy soft beds and fireplaces but the money he brought in would allow him to drape the siren and her lair with riches. It didn't take much to convince the avaricious siren of the benefits of this idea.

Yaris returned to Magnimar and managed to convince several investors that the rumors of Virashi were little more than that, and that he would be able to build a thriving settlement on the island. Once they arrived, he chose a site at the center of the island that overlooked the Varisian Gulf to serve as his new village's foundation, and commissioned the creation of several watchtowers and lighthouses to warn what he hoped would be a steady influx of merchant traffic away from the dangerous reefs.

The island's rugged terrain made farming impossible, so Yaris had shiploads of deer, boar, donkey rats, rabbits, and other animals brought and released in an attempt to seed a self-sustaining local wildlife population to help support his citizens. And as the money started flowing in, he made good on his promise and did indeed drape Virashi in riches.

Yet as the construction of Witchlight and the watchtowers continued, it became apparent that Yaris's dream was unraveling. What was initially intended to be a self-sustaining settlement became more and more reliant on supplies from Riddleport, and that city was only too eager to gouge Yaris for every penny. As dissent increased among his people, Yaris's bad luck seemed only to grow. The western watchtower burned partially to the ground only a week after construction was complete, killing nearly a dozen laborers and Yaris's brother in the process. Several weeks later, a ship bearing a huge shipment of grain ran afoul of the reefs surrounding the island, and the giant centipedes that had infested the ship made it ashore and quickly bloomed into one of the island's most obnoxious and dangerous pests. The spate of bad luck gave rise to whispers of "Virashi's Curse," and more and more locals began to speak of seeing a ghostly woman-faced bird in the forests and on the rocky shores. Yaris railed against these rumors, but was unable to offer proof that Virashi wasn't behind the "curse" without revealing his secret. Then, at the onset of winter during a particularly violent storm, the final blow struck. A shipment of diseased cattle brought to the island to augment meager food stores saw an outbreak of the deadly disease anthrakitis (see *Pathfinder #8*) that killed off a third of Witchlight's population. Distraught over the fact that his dream was falling apart, Yaris went down to seek comfort with Virashi—but he was followed by a suspicious priest who believed Yaris had made a deal with a devil that had gone sour. The priest's fears were confirmed when he witnessed Yaris and Virashi embrace. He returned to Witchlight, roused a mob, and under the protection of a *silence* spell, led the mob down to Virashi's cave the next morning and slew the siren as she slept in her lair.

Yaris woke the next day to a horrific sight—the body of his lover hanging from a pole above a fire in the middle of Witchlight. Overcome with grief and shock, Yaris threw himself from the eastern watchtower onto the rocks and surf below. This was the final blow to the settlement—without Yaris to provide encouragement, the remaining citizens of Devil's Elbow packed up and left for easier lives in Riddleport, Magnimar, or beyond. By the end of the week, Devil's Elbow had been abandoned.

For the past several decades, Devil's Elbow has remained uninhabited. Travelers on ships passing close to the island sometimes claim to see lights burning in the island's watchtowers, further inspiring rumors that the place is haunted. These rumors are given weight every few years when adventurers decide to sail out to the island in search of Virashi's hidden treasure, since many of them do not return, and those who do come with tales of monstrous centipedes, strange noises, and mysterious lights in the woods. This, combined with the fact that an unusual number of ships seem to wreck and sink in the waters within a 5-mile radius around the island, secured the region's ill repute, and today, very few visitors come to its deserted shores.

Recently, a new group has come to Devil's Elbow—the drow. They have selected the site as a testing ground for a terrible weapon, a weapon that calls down a meteor from the dark above and hurls it to earth. The weapon worked perfectly when they fired it, and the explosion was seen for miles around. Yet more than rock and fire fell from the sky that fateful night...

Adventure Synopsis

This adventure begins with the PCs traveling to the island of Devil's Elbow, either on their own to seek out their fortune in skymetal or at the behest of their new friend Kwava, who wants the PCs to follow up on rumors that the drow have established a base of operations there and may have had something to do with the recent falling star that struck the island.

The PCs arrive on the island only to find that the various groups of prospectors who arrived there before them have had a dreadful time, for there are more than drow on the island. The falling star carried with it dozens of cocooned aliens called akatas, and when the impact woke them, they swiftly infested the island. As the PCs explore Devil's Elbow, they'll find that one group of prospectors is waiting for them to hire their ship to return to Riddleport, another is trapped inside a ruined tower, a third has set up a camp to the east and is attempting to capture akatas for its own uses, and a fourth group has vanished entirely.

Eventually, through interactions with the various groups and a bit of exploration of their own, the PCs discover the drow hideout on the island. By defeating these drow, they recover several clues that point to the fact that the drow here were but a fraction of the total number now dwelling in the elven ruins of Celwynvian, and that the dark elves' plan may be more threatening than imagined.

PART ONE: THE GREAT SKYMETAL RUSH

As "Children of the Void" begins, Riddleport is on the mend from the destructive climax that closed out the previous adventure. The mysterious shadow in the sky is

gone, and the strange events that have been plaguing the city have ended. The falling star that struck Devil's Elbow is now accepted by both commonfolk and cyphermages alike as having been the cause of these disturbances, and now that it has fallen to Golarion, the feelings of nervous fear have passed.

Indeed, it was the effects of the relatively small (but still destructive) tsunami that hit Riddleport after the star crashed that have been on the minds of the city's denizens recently. When the wave surged ashore, dozens of ships were beached, with several washed inland and left stranded as far as Wharf Street. Many of Riddleport's piers were ruined, and several of the smaller buildings along the waterfront were damaged. Over the days following the event, the crimelords and overlord of Riddleport mobilized in a way rarely seen in the lawless city, working together to put out fires, save citizens who were swept out into the harbor, and kill angry and disoriented reefclaws, sharks, bunyips, and other dangerous sea creatures that suddenly found themselves stranded in the city streets.

In the aftermath, the cost of the damage to buildings and structures rises into the tens of thousands of gold, and the total number slain or swept out to sea by the wave may never be known (thanks to the city's inefficient census practices), although the more conservative estimates place the total number of victims between 150 to 200. Yet despite the disaster, Riddleport is quick to forget the trauma. Those who weren't directly harmed by the wave have little compassion for those who do, while those who were affected are universally quick to turn the event from disaster into opportunity. In the days and weeks to follow, the chaos on the waterfront makes for ripe grounds for smugglers, looters, and other violent criminals. Ships that were further out to sea return to find many of their competitors no longer in a position to work against them, and the balance of power among the various pirate captains has shifted dramatically (not that many outside of that violent subculture would notice much difference).

In addition, with each passing day, a new greed continues to grow among Riddleport's citizens—a greed for skymetal. After the initial shock of the falling star and its impact subsided, the implications of the event sunk in. Skymetal, in any of its seven known varieties, is a valued and much sought-after commodity in any society, but with Riddleport's Gas Forges being one of Varisia's only public operations capable of smelting such difficult metals, the convenience of the fallen star has many of Riddleport's groups eager for a chance at the easy money.

Yet the damage done to Riddleport's waterfront and to many of the ships owned by prominent locals has retarded the burgeoning Skymetal Rush. As the days drag on, the race to be the first to reach Devil's Elbow slowly takes the city by storm, with those who don't have access to ships scrambling to secure deals with those who do. But the promise of skymetal is not the only thing that waits on Devil's Elbow—for at the end of the previous adventure, the PCs likely learned that the falling star was called down by the drow, and that those drow might still be hiding somewhere on the island.

The Gold Goblin Gambling Hall

The PCs might find themselves in an unusual situation at the start of this adventure—they might be the newest owners of the Gold Goblin Gaming Hall. Assuming the PCs don't want to retire from the adventuring life, this essentially leaves them with two options.

Selling Off: If the PCs wish to sell the Gold Goblin, they'll find the task isn't as easy as simply finding a buyer. Recent events at the gambling hall (including several raids and fights) have led to a public conception that the place is bad luck, so even if the PCs had helped nurse the Gold Goblin into profitability in the previous adventure, finding a buyer willing to pay a fair price may be difficult. Once the PCs indicate that the Gold Goblin is for sale, allow one of them to attempt a DC 20 Diplomacy check each week (other PCs can attempt to aid another on this roll if they spend at least 8 hours over the course of that week spreading the word). Although the building itself is worth quite a lot, hidden fees such as taxes due to the overlord, along with payments and bribes to various guilds and crime lords, do quite an effective job chipping away at potential profit. After all is said and done, the most the PCs can hope to make from selling the Gold Goblin is about 20,000 gp, although no one in Riddleport is ready to pay all of that at once. A good down payment is anywhere between 5,000 and 8,000 gp—let the PCs set the methods of payments as they will (most buyers will balk at anything more than 1,000 gp a month, and would vastly prefer something closer to 200 to 500 gp a month), and don't be afraid to have whoever they sell try to eventually use trickery or even murder to try to get out of making all of the payments that are due—this is Riddleport, after all!

Business Owners: If the PCs decide to keep the Gold Goblin, they don't necessarily have to stay on site to continue making money off the venture. "Shadow in the Sky" presented a method to track the Gold Goblin's profitability, but now that the PCs are the owners, they not only enjoy all of the profit (rather than just a weekly bonus to their wages) but also have to shoulder all of the costs. Since the focus of Second Darkness isn't running a gambling hall, the following simplified system should do to determine how much money the venture makes each month.

Costs: It costs at least 200 gp a month to run the Gold Goblin, combining all of the necessary wages to workers,

DOWN TIME

The time it takes Riddleport to recover from the tsunami to a point where this adventure begins is kept fluid—you can have this period last as long as you and your players wish. After the end of the previous adventure, the players may be ready to sail to Devil's Elbow immediately to follow up on what they read in Depora's journal. Alternatively, they might want to spend some time recovering and running business at the Gold Goblin. When you feel the PCs are ready to head into this adventure, then and only then is the right time to have Kwava approach the PCs with his proposal and get this adventure moving.

taxes and bribes, repairs, and necessary reserves to cover day-to-day payouts of customer winnings at the games. If the PCs aren't there to run the place themselves, they'll want to hire managers to handle the business for them, which increases the monthly costs to 300 gp. Every month, there's a 20% chance that unexpected costs appear in the form of bail for employees, particularly large repairs, or unexpectedly lucky customers—if there are unexpected costs, increase that month's costs by 1d6×10% of the normal costs.

Profits: Running the Gold Goblin requires its owner or manager to be on site 6 days a week for a minimum of 8 hours a day. At the end of a month, the owner or manager makes a Profession (bookkeeper, gambler, innkeeper, or tavern keeper) check and multiplies the result of his check by 20. The resulting number is how much gold the gambling hall takes in during that month; subtract the month's costs to determine actual profits for the month. Any month in which the profits are negative indicate a loss. If that loss isn't paid by the PCs by the time the next month comes, the entire staff quits and the building is abandoned. If the PCs aren't there to fix things, Overlord Cromarcky is swift to step in and claim the building as his own property, at which point reclaiming ownership may be impossible without a fight or a lot of money.

If the PCs hire managers to run the business, assume they have Profession (gambler) +8 for the purposes of determining the Gold Goblin's monthly profits.

Implications

At the end of the previous adventure, the PCs are hit with two relatively major discoveries. The most sensational is that the drow are somehow involved with the falling star that struck Devil's Elbow. But while this is a shock, to the people of Riddleport the revelation that the drow are, in fact, *real* could be an even larger surprise.

Drow have long been a part of the RPG tradition, but until this Adventure Path, no *Pathfinder Chronicles* product has included them as villains—this is by design.

The drow of Golarion are, to most of the surface dwelling world, unsubstantiated legends. The rare few incidents in which they've appeared on the surface have been handled swiftly by a powerful and secretive society of elves based in the nation of Kyonin—this society is the Winter Council, and it is primarily due to their actions that the truth behind the legends of dark elves has remained just that. Yet now the Winter Council is fractured, their once clockwork-like precision compromised from within. As Second Darkness progresses, word that the drow exist spreads, and the PCs are destined to be at the forefront of that storm.

How this storm hits Riddleport depends in large part on how the PCs' fight with Depora went in the previous adventure. If they defeated her in the caves and didn't tell anyone about her presence, then they unwittingly served the Winter Council's desires and prevented the news from spreading. If, on the other hand, the PCs make an effort to spread knowledge about the drow's presence, or more likely, their final fight with Depora brought them out into the open and culminated atop the Cyphergate for all of Riddleport to see, rumors of drow involvement with the falling star and the tsunami that struck Riddleport quickly take root— for certainly these two major revelations are not unconnected...

Kwava

Adventure Hooks

"Children of the Void" allows you and your players some leeway in how to begin. Depending on how the PCs react to the information they recovered at the end of "Shadow in the Sky" or the burgeoning greed for skymetal, they may well create their own adventure hooks. If the PCs have forged close associations with one of the four initial prospecting groups, they may be called upon to go to Devil's Elbow to check up on them after the initial group hasn't been heard from. Alternatively, the PCs could simply decide to form their own prospecting group and might charter a boat to Devil's Elbow to see about making their own fortunes with skymetal.

However, this adventure assumes that the primary reason the PCs travel to Devil's Elbow is to follow up on what they learned from Depora Azrinae's journal—the notion that there could be more drow hidden on Devil's Elbow, and that they may have had something to do with the falling star, should be enough to pique interest. It's certainly enough to intrigue one of the PCs' allies, Kwava, if he finds out—the following adventure hook is thus the one this adventure assumes.

Kwava's Request: In "Shadow in the Sky," the PCs met an unusual elf by the name of Kwava, likely just before they were ambushed by a group of wererats. Kwava is an elf from the distant Ekujae tribe of the Mwangi Expanse far to the south, a ranger who traveled north to seek his destiny. Not long after coming to the town of Crying Leaf in northwestern Varisia, Kwava joined a mercenary group called the Shin'Rakorath, one of the Winter Council's many subgroups used, secretly, to combat the emergence of the drow. Only long-time members of the Shin'Rakorath know the truth about the drow—new recruits like Kwava generally have to go through a period of apprenticeship lasting for decades before their superiors trust them enough to reveal the organization's true motives. The Shin'Rakorath know that the drow have a strong presence in northwestern Varisia (particularly in the ruined elven city of Celwynvian), but they have recently come to fear that the drow have been extending their taint through other nearby regions as well. Short on agents, the mercenary leaders sent many recruits into the surrounding areas with orders to seek out rumors of "renegade elves" that may indicate drow activity. Kwava's orders brought him to Riddleport, where he soon learned that a man named Saul Vancaskerkin had joined forces with one such renegade elf. He allied with the PCs when Saul attempted to have them ambushed and killed by wererats, and by the end of the previous adventure, the PCs should count him as an ally.

Once word gets out that a drow was sighted in Riddleport, the Shin'Rakorath moves quickly. Kwava is contacted by his superiors via *animal messenger* and is told to follow up on the drow, to find out what she was doing in Riddleport, and to make sure she was the only one active. Kwava's first step in this mission is to contact the PCs and ask them to share everything they've learned about Depora and her plans. Why was she in Riddleport? Does she have allies?

If Kwava learns (or suspects) there are more drow on Devil's Elbow, he reports the news quickly to his superiors via *animal messenger*. The reply comes in about 8 hours later via another *animal messenger* delivery—the Shin'Rakorath wants him to continue his investigation, but urges him to draw upon the PCs as additional aid, particularly in exploring the possibility of there being more drow on Devil's Elbow. The message goes on to say that the Shin'Rakorath has even gone so far as to arrange for transportation to the island via a ship called the *Flying Cloud*. They'll send more agents south to Riddleport to help as soon as they can, but for the immediate future their hands are tied with events in Celwynvian and the Mierani Forest—it could be weeks or even months before they can spare anyone to aid in the investigation of Devil's Elbow.

Kwava would rather remain in the Riddleport hinterlands at this time so he'll be available to his superiors should they need to contact him, but if the PCs want him to come along (and you feel that they could use a little extra help during the adventure), he can certainly accompany them to Devil's Elbow to provide a little more support against the perils that await there.

The Prospectors

Although estimations of how much skymetal is just lying around on Devil's Elbow waiting to be picked up off the ground seems to be the favored topic of conversation, very few in Riddleport can actually get to the island with anything approaching speed. Several groups, however, do have the resources to mount just such an expedition, and only a few days after the star fell, the race to be the first group to Devil's Elbow began!

Each of the following five groups (one being an optional group) has its own specific goals and fate on Devil's Elbow. The PCs' group is the last of these to arrive. If the PCs wish to do a little asking around to find out what groups are interested in the island (and thus what groups they might come into conflict with), a Gather Information check reveals information about all of the groups that the check's result exceeds.

DC 10—Goldhammer's Expedition: Since Overlord Cromarcky hired several dwarves to sail out to Devil's Elbow to gather up as much skymetal as possible for him, everyone's heard about the interest the dwarves of the Gas Forges have in the fallen star. The dwarves, led by a loud miner named Goldhammer, left for Devil's Elbow 2 days before the start of this adventure on a ship named the *Mithral Wave*, which dropped the dwarves off and then sailed on to make a delivery to Magnimar—the plan is to pick up the dwarves on the return trip in a week.

DC 12—Slyeg's Group: Avery Slyeg, Riddleport's most successful smuggler and black marketeer, was the first to act on the promise of skymetal. With one of his ships not quite in port when the star fell, he was able to move quickly when the *Black Bunyip* returned to Riddleport. Avery outfitted her quickly, and his group of smugglers and thugs left for Devil's Elbow 7 days before the start of this adventure.

DC 15—Cyphermages: Eager to investigate the island but frustrated by attempts to organize transport (due to a combination of internal bickering and the sabotage

efforts of Zincher's men), the cyphermages finally secured a small group of a dozen or so explorers and secured passage to the island on the *Foamrunner*, a merchant cog bound for Magnimar. The cyphermages left for Devil's Elbow 3 days ago. Samaritha Beldusk is among those who travel to the island on the *Foamrunner*, and if she's in a relationship with a PC, she sends a note to that PC informing him or her of what she's doing, assuring the PC that she'll return safe and sound in a few weeks.

DC 18—Zincher's Group: Clegg Zincher didn't have the luxury of a ship returning to port, nor did he have Overlord Cromarcky's finances to rush repairs on one of his own vessels. Nor does he trust his men not to simply gather the skymetal and run with it. Zincher waited for the next pirate ship to pull into port, then personally led a hand-picked crew of toughs down to the waterfront that evening to attack the ship under the cover of night. After murdering the crew and feeding them to the hungry harbor denizens, Zincher and his crew sailed the stolen *Dark Pearl* out to Devil's Elbow 5 days before the start of this adventure.

DC 20—Pirates: If you wish to use "Teeth of Araska," this volume's Set-Piece adventure, then the pirate ship has anchored off the eastern shore of Devil's Elbow. Further information on how to include this ship as a part of the adventure appears on page 64. Numerous options are presented, some requiring the pirates to precede the PCs.

The Flying Cloud

Whatever reason the PCs settle on for visiting Devil's Elbow, they'll need to secure passage to the island (which is a good 18 miles away from Riddleport) on a ship. After the tsunami, many of Riddleport's vessels were damaged, and those that were repaired first were done so with financing from the Order of Cyphers, Clegg Zincher, and the Gas Forge. Yet other ships soon become available—and the first one that does so for the PCs is a fast ship called the *Flying Cloud*. This ship's captain is an adventurer named Josper Creesy, a man who hopes to set a record for speed sailing from Varisia all the way to distant Andoran. Just recently returned from a "practice run" from Riddleport to Magnimar and back, he's intrigued to learn of the recent events (although the falling star was impressive, it went largely unnoticed by the Lost Coast and Magnimar 200 or so miles to the south), and anyone who approaches him with a request to sail out to Devil's Elbow to investigate finds him easy to convince.

Whoever the PCs are working for (again, this adventure assumes they're working with the Shin'Rakorath, with Kwava as intermediary), the *Flying Cloud* should be the best choice the PCs have for getting to the island. If they decide

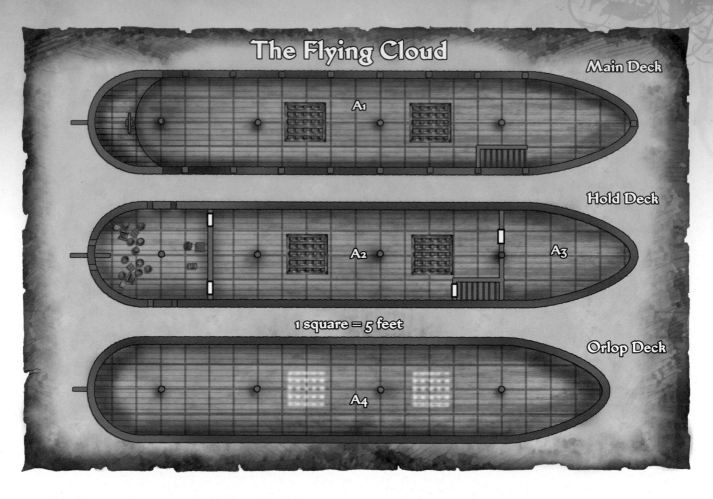

The Flying Cloud

Main Deck

A1

Hold Deck

A2

A3

1 square = 5 feet

Orlop Deck

A4

for whatever reason not to take the *Flying Cloud*, the easiest solution is to simply give them another ship name but still use the information presented here. If the PCs are working with the Shin'Rakorath, they send Kwava the necessary funds to hire a ship, but if the PCs are on their own, they'll need to come up with the 50 gp necessary to secure passage to the small island (this cost is significantly higher than normal, since it involves some risk to the ship, although it does cover the entire party's fare along with any mounts they wish to transport).

The *Flying Cloud* is a four-masted vessel built for speed. With a narrow beam, sharply raked stem, and square rig, the distinctive design (itself based on the design of the larger Chelish clipper) gives the ship great speed on the waves when under full sail. The *Flying Cloud* flies the flag of Riddleport on her mainmast (although the captain keeps a dozen flags in storage and feels no real ties to any one port). Captain Josper Creesy, a relatively young man, seeks to make a name for himself and his ship by setting speed records all along the Arcadian Coast.

A1. Main Deck: The *Flying Cloud's* main deck has no forecastle or cabin, but a slightly raised and uncovered quarterdeck gives the captain a better view of the seas ahead and a modicum of protection from the elements.

Two hatches open to the lower decks—10-foot-square openings that allow for the loading of cargo into the hold below. Each hatch is fitted with ladders to allow the crew and passengers a route between decks. A narrow flight of stairs leads down from the bow to the lower deck as well.

A2. Galley and Hold: This large space acts as both galley and hold. A few bunks built along the hull provide relatively comfortable sleeping arrangements for the crew, leaving the central reach for cargo, taking meals, or just relaxing. Ladders connected to the hatches provide access both to the main deck above and the orlop deck below. The main hold is currently empty of cargo. A smaller hold toward the ship's stern contains foodstuffs, tools, sails, chains, rope, timbers, and other materials necessary for at-sea repairs.

A3. Cabin: This room serves as the captain's cabin and private dining area. A table with several chairs (enough for the captain and the PCs), a desk, and a large bunk comprise the furniture here.

A4. Orlop Deck: The low-clearance orlop deck holds the ship's supplies and provides additional containment space for large cargos. Food, fresh water, ropes, tools, and repair materials are lashed and stowed on this deck, but there is nothing of interest here. Medium characters

moving around in the orlop deck find it cramped and fight with a –2 penalty on attack rolls.

Sabotage! (EL 4)

Captain Creesy invites the PCs to dine with him aboard the *Flying Cloud* the night before they are set to embark—he wishes to get to know them a little and find out why they're heading to Devil's Elbow, and during the dinner he all but interrogates them on their goals and plans once they arrive at the island. Captain Creesy's initial attitude toward the PCs is indifferent—during the dinner, have the PC with the highest Diplomacy check roll to see if the captain can be made friendlier (other PCs can attempt to aid another with their own Diplomacy checks). If the PCs make him friendly, he warms to them and his interrogation swiftly transforms into actual conversation. He's eager to talk about his desire to set sailing speed records between Varisia and Andoran, but admits he's still months away from making the attempt. A local, Captain Creesy is well-versed in the stories of the region, and if the PCs don't already know the history

of Devil's Elbow or Virashi's Curse, Creesy is only too eager to tell them the story of how Yaris's attempt to settle on Devil's Elbow fell apart, it is said, due to the siren's curse. If made helpful, Creesy befriends the PCs and he waives his 50 gp fee to transport them and their gear to Devil's Elbow.

Creesy and the PCs dine belowdecks in the captain's cabin, where he treats the PCs to a fine meal of fresh reefclaw and vegetables with warm bread and chilled wine. He makes a quip to them to not get used to such finery once the ship is underway, but for now they should enjoy the meal.

Creatures: Unfortunately, the PCs' preparations for the journey to Devil's Elbow have not gone unnoticed. A group of six saboteurs employed by Clegg Zincher have taken note of the *Flying Cloud*'s preparation for sail the next morning, and after some well-placed bribes, they learn that it is bound for Devil's Elbow. While the PCs and Captain Creesy eat, the saboteurs slip onto the ship and begin their dirty work, first subduing the two guards Creesy's left up topside and then preparing to burn the ship's sails and rigging.

Allow Captain Creesy and the PCs to make Listen checks to notice the scuffle, opposed by the saboteurs' +8 Move Silently bonus (apply an extra +10 bonus to the saboteurs' Move Silently checks in this instance due to distance and one closed door between them and the PCs).

If the PCs don't hear them, the saboteurs pour oil over the rigging and sails of the ship and light them up with vials of alchemist's fire. The saboteurs need only 2 rounds to spread the proper amount of oil, then they throw down their alchemist's fire on round 3. Once the saboteurs succeed in igniting the rigging and sails, they stay and watch for 3 rounds to make sure the fire has truly caught before they retreat down to the pier and up onto the waterfront boardwalk. Give the PCs a DC 20 Listen check every round after the fire starts to hear the flames. If they do not succeed by the 4th round of the fire, they'll automatically hear the warning cry from a nearby ship: "Fire! Fire at the docks!"

The standard response in Riddleport to a burning ship is to simply cut the mooring lines and let the ship drift into the harbor and burn to the waterline. The six saboteurs do this as soon as the warning cry goes up, posing as concerned citizens (although a DC 10 Sense Motive check is enough to correctly deduce the nature of their barely-concealed laughter as they work). Left to drift, the *Flying Cloud* burns to the waterline in 5d6 minutes. Any attempt to fight the flames before the critical first 5 minutes pass can stop the fire before it spreads to the ship itself, resulting in merely damaged sails and rigging (which can be replaced with a day's work and 15 gp of repair materials); otherwise, the ship is lost unless magic like *pyrotechnics* or *quench* is used to put out the fire.

Captain Josper Creesy — CR 4
Male human expert 4/fighter 1
CG Medium humanoid
Init +7; **Senses** Listen −1, Spot −1

DEFENSE
AC 17, touch 13, flat-footed 14
    (+3 armor, +3 Dex, +1 shield)
hp 27 (5 HD; 4d6+1d10+5)
Fort +4, **Ref** +4, **Will** +3

OFFENSE
Spd 30 ft.

Melee mwk sap +9 (1d6+1 nonlethal) or
    rapier +7 (1d6+1/18–20)
Ranged light crossbow +7 (1d8/19–20)

TACTICS
During Combat Captain Creesy generally doesn't fight to kill, preferring to use his sap in combat against malcontent crewmen, saboteurs, or any other foe he encounters. The one way to ensure his wrath is to damage his ship—in that case, Creesy isn't above using his crossbow or rapier to finish off his enemies.
Morale Captain Creesy flees if reduced to 10 or fewer hit points unless he's fighting to defend his ship, in which case he fights to the death.

STATISTICS
Str 12, **Dex** 16, **Con** 13, **Int** 10, **Wis** 8, **Cha** 14
Base Atk +4; **Grp** +5
Feats Improved Initiative, Skill Focus (Profession [sailor]), Weapon Finesse, Weapon Focus (sap)
Skills Balance +12, Climb +9, Intimidate +10, Profession (sailor) +9, Tumble +10, Swim +9, Use Rope +8
Languages Common, Varisian
Combat Gear *potion of cure moderate wounds* (2), *potion of water breathing*; **Other Gear** +1 *leather armor*, buckler, masterwork sap, rapier, light crossbow with 10 bolts

Captain Josper Creesy

Saboteurs (6) — CR 1
Human rogue 1
NE Medium humanoid
Init +6; **Senses** Listen +4, Spot +4

DEFENSE
AC 15, touch 12, flat-footed 13
    (+3 armor, +2 Dex)
hp 8 (1d6+2)
Fort +2, **Ref** +4, **Will** +0

OFFENSE
Spd 30 ft.
Melee short sword +1 (1d6+1/19–20)
Ranged light crossbow +2 (1d8/19–20)
Special Attacks sneak attack +1d6

TACTICS
During Combat The saboteurs realize they are outmatched by the PCs, so they work to avoid melee combat as much as possible, using one or two of their number to hold off any melee fighters if they need to while the others attack with their hand crossbows.
Morale The saboteurs came to burn a ship, not fight against experienced adventurers. If a saboteur takes any

damage at all, he attempts to flee (including jumping overboard and swimming away, although there's a 25% chance per jumper that a shark, reefclaw, bunyip, or other dangerous predator is nearby and attacks before he can reach the shore). If a saboteur can't flee without provoking an attack of opportunity, he instead drops his weapon and begs for his life.

STATISTICS

Str 13, **Dex** 15, **Con** 14, **Int** 12, **Wis** 10, **Cha** 8

Base Atk +0; **Grp** +1

Feats Improved Initiative, Stealthy

Skills Bluff +3, Disable Device +5, Hide +8, Intimidate +3, Knowledge (local) +5, Listen +4, Move Silently +8, Open Lock +6, Sleight of Hand +6, Spot +4

Languages Common, Varisian

SQ trapfinding

Combat Gear alchemist's fire (2); **Other Gear** masterwork studded leather, short sword, light crossbow with 10 bolts

Development: If the PCs capture one or more of the saboteurs, they can try to get some information. The saboteurs are initially unfriendly, but if made at least friendly (via Diplomacy or Intimidate), they talk—although if they do, they try to answer questions with as little information as possible. At first, they try to Bluff the PCs into believing that they were simply engaging in some idle vandalism, but any real threat or pressure at this point gets them to admit that they were paid a total of 20 gp apiece by Clegg Zincher to make sure that no other ships bound for Devil's Elbow set out until, at the very least, the end of the month. The saboteurs assume that Zincher simply wants to limit the amount of competition for skymetal harvesting, but beyond this, they know little more of interest.

PART TWO: DEVIL'S ELBOW

Located 18 miles southwest of Riddleport and a mere 2 miles from the rugged and wild cliff shores of the Calphiak Mountains, the 5-mile-wide island of Devil's Elbow appears on few maps. Its relatively remote location and notorious history have worked well together to ensure that it has remained mostly abandoned after an attempt to establish a settlement on its southern ridge (as summarized in the Adventure Background).

Adventure Timeline

Although the PCs are free to explore Devil's Elbow at their leisure, several key events occur before their arrival on the notorious island. These events are presented in a timeline below, but exact dates are not given so you can time this adventure as best fits your campaign.

Several Months Ago: As the grand weapon nears completion, a group of drow led by Depora Azrinae comes to Devil's Elbow to set up the island as a testing ground. They move into Virashi's caves, encounter the siren's ghost and imprison her in her cave, and then expand a tunnel that leads north to a point about a mile and a half to the northwest. They create a large chamber underground there and begin the process of crafting the intricate glyphs that will call down a star from the sky.

One Month Ago: The drow complete the glyphs. Depora Azrinae relocates to Riddleport to pursue other goals, and the two drow wizards who constructed the glyphs return to Celwynvian—neither of these higher-ranking drow have any real interest in being so close to ground-zero when the star hits. A small contingent of drow, including the eccentric druid Xakihn and a priestess of Nocticula named Shindiira, remain behind to guard the site while the glyphs begin the weeks-long process of charging before they fire.

Over a Week Ago: The weapon fires, and a falling star strikes Devil's Elbow. As the meteor scythes through the sky, fragments break away to pepper the surrounding area; one primary blast hits the island and several smaller fragments strike elsewhere. Most of these fragments contain cocoons made of noqual that hold slumbering creatures known as akatas. Many of these dangerous predators hatch over the course of the next several days, beginning their destructive life cycle and growing to maturity not long before the PCs arrive on the island.

One Week Ago: A few days after the incident but a few hours before the first group of prospectors arrives, the drow finish gathering up the larger remnants of the meteorite from the primary crater and they return them to their cave. Slyeg's men arrive on the island in the evening and that night encounter drow and are slain. The drow use the bodies of these men to study the effects akata larvae have upon the dead, creating several dangerous undead known as void zombies that the drow then release into the wild.

Five Days Ago: Zincher's group arrives at Devil's Elbow and finds the *Black Bunyip* apparently abandoned in the island's only harbor. Zincher seizes the ship and spends part of the day searching for Slyeg's men; when he doesn't find them, he orders a third of his men to remain with him on the island while the others sail the *Black Bunyip* (with his own *Dark Pearl* as an escort) to Roderic's Cove to have the ship refit and rebuilt (doing so in Riddleport carrying with it a much increased risk of Slyeg noticing the theft) so that Zincher can claim it as his own property and Slyeg won't even recognize it as his own. The refitting will take 2 weeks, at which point Zincher's prepared to return to Riddleport a rich man with two ships filled with skymetal.

Four Days Ago: Zincher is charmed by Shindiira Misraria, who then orders him to use his men as guardians for the drow while they finish their observations of the captured akatas and the harvested skymetal. Zincher moves his camp from Witchlight to a new site to the southwest, just above the hidden path down to the drow caves, so he can be in closer contact to his new allies.

Three Days Ago: The cyphermages, led by a wizard named Fenella, arrive on the island. They avoid Zincher's crew and set up their camp in Witchlight.

Two Days Ago: The Goldhammer Expedition arrives and has a brief meeting with the cyphermages when they find the best site for a base already occupied. When the cyphermages refuse to share the site, the resentful dwarves are forced to settle for the pier area.

Yesterday: The akata population reaches critical mass on the island, and a large number of the creatures attack the cyphermages. Several of them, including Fenella, are killed, and the remaining cyphermages retreat to the central watchtower to regroup and plan an escape. The dwarves suffer a similar fate, but they never quite determine what exactly has been picking them off.

Today: The PCs arrive on the island.

Landfall on Devil's Elbow

Repairs delay the initial plan to leave Riddleport for Devil's Elbow, but assuming the PCs stopped the saboteurs or put out the fire before it could spread from the rigging and sails, the delay is only a few hours. By early afternoon, the *Flying Cloud* is ready to set sail for Devil's Elbow. The journey is short, and the ship covers the 18-mile voyage in a mere 5 hours, reaching the island about an hour before sundown.

The forested island is quiet as the ship approaches; no signs of life are immediately apparent. A low ridge forms a spine along the length of the island, its slopes covered with dense forest and its shores affording very few safe places to land. Two stone towers rise above the level of the surrounding trees along the top of the island's ridge, one to the east and one at the island's center. If the PCs approach by day, a thin plume of smoke rises from a point about midway between those two towers at the height of the island's ridge. Yet the most dramatic sight as the ship nears its destination is the immense crater on the island's northeastern slopes. The crater itself is hundreds of feet wide and surrounded by an even larger swath of burnt trees that have been knocked flat

in a burst pattern around the impact site. The region's frequent rainstorms and damp conditions prevented the fire from consuming the entire island, yet in all nearly a quarter of the island's forest was destroyed by the impact.

Captain Creesy seems unusually nervous as the ship nears the island; despite his bravado, the tales of Virashi's Curse and the island's history get to him, and the sight of the immense crater does little to calm his nerves. He tells the PCs that he'd rather not stay in the region, and he attempts to arrange for a pick-up date when they'll be done and he can come back and collect them. As he speaks, a bright light suddenly flashes at the peak of the island's central tower, a sparkling blast of *pyrotechnics* that lasts for several seconds before expiring. The mysterious flash of light seals the deal—Creesy will sail up to the old piers at area **A** and allow the PCs to disembark, but he does not want to remain overnight within sight of the island.

Creesy is reluctant to dock anywhere but at area **A** due to the dangerous reefs. Only a few minutes after the ship docks and the PCs are unloading any gear and mounts they brought with them, a voice calls out from the seemingly abandoned buildings: "Ahoy, the ship! Ahoy! Goldhammer's Expedition requesting permission to approach!" The speaker is **Gravin Goldhammer** (N dwarf aristocrat 2/expert 2), leader of his eponymous expedition and official representative of the Gas Forges. As the dwarf nears the docks, followed by four others (two dwarves and two humans), it should be apparent to the PCs that they've had a rough time. Their clothes are torn and filthy and their faces are tired and haggard. Only these four of Gravin's original dozen expedition members remain alive, and they've had enough of "this cursed island." They seek passage on the *Flying Cloud* to return to Riddleport. The dwarves begin as friendly, assuming the PCs treat them reasonably well. Captain Creesy is only too willing to take the dwarves up on their request for passage back to Riddleport, since it gives him an excuse to leave the island in his wake. Fortunately for the PCs, the captain doesn't intend to totally abandon them; he'll agree to come back to the docks here at any point in the future the PCs request (although the earliest he'll be able to return is tomorrow evening).

Gravin
Goldhammer

As the PCs offload and the terrified men clamber up onto the *Flying Cloud*, Gravin is willing to answer some questions the PCs might have of him. Likely questions, and his answers, are listed below.

Who are you? "My name is Gravin Goldhammer, the leader of this fool-fated expedition. We've only been here a couple days, and this is all what's left of the thirteen who landed."

What happened to you? "Them stories about Virashi's Curse are right—mostly. Only it ain't ghosts what haunt this place, no. It's monsters. Low-to-the-ground things, fast and lean. Never did get me a good look at one of them, even with them snatching a few of my men and dragging them off into the woods. A few others got bit or slashed, and their wounds turned bad. Some sort of sick got in them, and then, when they died, it came back out their faces. Torag's scars, but that were a sight I'd like to unsee. Came right out of their faces like they were tongues, and then my own men attacked us. We put them down and burned the bodies just this morning. Whatever's out there, it's not fit for this world. You shouldn't stay here. If you had any sense, you'd get back on that boat and head right back to Riddleport!"

Why are you here? "We came looking for skymetal, of course. Overlord Cromarcky hired my boss to send us out here. Unfortunately, we got here too late."

Why were you too late?/How much skymetal did you find? "Not a speck. Plenty of craters around, but nothing in them worth taking. Either the other groups got it all, or there wasn't any to begin with."

What other groups? "There's supposed to be three other groups here, but I only seen one of them so far—the cyphermages who are up in Witchlight. Slyeg and Zincher supposedly have men here too, but I ain't seen any of them... although we did spot some smoke rising to the southeast, like maybe from campfires."

What made that flash of light up on the hill? "My guess? One of them cyphermages. They settled in up there in the ruins of Witchlight and didn't want company. They've been doing that light stuff since last night—I sent four men up the hill to investigate, but I haven't seen any sign of them since. Whatever it is that's been picking us off must'a got them, and sure as my beard it's after the cyphermages too. Those flashes of light, I reckon, are calls for help. I've wasted enough of my men trying to answer that call, though. But hey, if you're heading up there, do me a favor. You find any of my men, try to see that they make it back to Riddleport, will ya? I'll put in a good word with the boss for a reward of a couple hundred gold if you do."

Have you seen any dark elves on the island? This question causes Goldhammer to make an exasperated expression before he answers. "Nope. No leprechauns or two-headed donkey rats either. We haven't even seen the Sandpoint Devil. You're welcome to look for all three, and dark elves as well, but I ain't staying here longer to see what other fanciful beasts this place has to offer."

Nothing can convince Gravin to stay on shore, and as soon as the PCs finish questioning him, he retreats belowdecks with his men—he doesn't come back up until the *Flying Cloud's* safely back in Riddleport.

Exploring Devil's Elbow

How the PCs handle the situation on Devil's Elbow is up to them, as is the order in which they explore the place. Somewhat overgrown roads still remain from the initial attempt to settle Devil's Elbow, and although the once wide roads have overgrown to little more than trails, these trails remain the easiest method to travel on Devil's Elbow. Moving along a trail can be done at normal speed, but once one moves off the trail into the densely forested slopes of the island, overland travel speed is cut in half, and the thick underbrush is treated as difficult terrain.

As the PCs explore the area, check for wandering monsters as indicated at the start of the Bestiary on page 78. The weather should remain overcast and glum for the duration of the PCs' stay on Devil's Elbow, raining two or three times a day for 10 to 20 minutes, perhaps for a few hours each night.

There are seven major encounter areas on Devil's Elbow, each of which are detailed here. Of the seven, three (Witchlight, Zincher's Camp, and the Sea Caves) comprise the three major encounter areas in the adventure; these three locations are detailed in Parts Three, Four, and Five. The PCs can investigate these locations in any order they wish, although the layout of the island and the hidden nature of the sea caves make it likely that the PCs tackle them in the order presented.

While there are several minor goals for the PCs to realize during this adventure (such as rescuing Samaritha, defeating Clegg, and discovering the secret of Virashi's Curse and the location of her treasure), the primary goal is the recovery of the documents in area **G9g**. With these key documents, the elves of Crying Leaf will finally have the edge they need to drive the drow from Celwynvian—these documents are thus the "key" into the next adventure in this campaign. As soon as the PCs recover these documents, they should be ready to move on to the next adventure—but if they wish to remain on Devil's Elbow a while longer to tie up a few loose ends, by all means, let them!

Lesser Craters

The huge crater visible from sea on the island's northeast slopes isn't the only one on Devil's Elbow. Several smaller

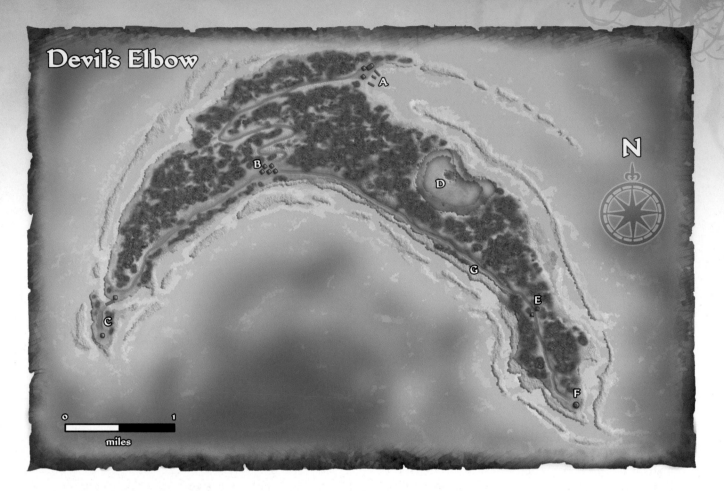

Devil's Elbow

N

0 — 1
miles

craters pock the island as well, although they're well hidden by surrounding terrain as the destruction created by their impact was relatively minor. A character has a 20% chance per 8 hours spent exploring the island of stumbling across one of these craters. Each of these craters was made by a fragment of the larger meteorite, and each had several akata cocoons embedded in it. The hatching of these cocoons resulted in the majority of the wild akatas now loose on the island. A 10-minute DC 25 Search check of a crater has a 20% chance of revealing 1d3 pounds of noqual skymetal (see page 19 for details). A single lesser crater can yield no more than 5 pounds in all over the course of several searches.

A. Harbor

When Yaris Neraken first attempted to settle Devil's Elbow, the three piers and houses here were the first structures he built, since they would serve as the gateway between Witchlight and the rest of the world. Situated in the only safe harbor on the island's shore, the buildings here once served as warehouses and homes for guards and laborers, but they are now long abandoned and partially collapsed due to the falling star; little remains of the buildings but heaps of rubble and a few leaning walls. Likewise, the piers themselves

are falling into disrepair, with many planks missing from their lengths, especially at the ends where only a few leaning pilings protrude from the surf. There's nothing unusual or particularly interesting in the ruined buildings, with the exception of several bright red, foot-long centipedes that scurry for cover as soon as anyone approaches.

B. Witchlight

Reaching Witchlight requires a difficult slog up a steep, overgrown trail that winds up the mountainous island, or an even more difficult slog up through dense underbrush. Witchlight itself is located atop the island's highest peak, affording a peerless view of the Varisian Gulf. On particularly clear days, the distant haze of Riddleport can be seen to the northeast.

Currently, Witchlight is the site of a massacre. Turkey vultures wheel in the sky above, and the lights that periodically flash from its tower are desperate attempts by the cyphermages trapped there to call for help. The abandoned settlement is detailed further in Part Three.

C. Western Lighthouse (EL 5)

Originally intended to be one of three watchtowers and lighthouses, tragedy struck this building days after it was completed. The fire partially burnt the building and resulted in the deaths of several workers, forcing Yaris to abandon the site. Although he intended to rebuild, he never got the chance. Now, time and the recent impact have finished the job; the tower has fallen completely into a huge mound of rubble.

Creatures: The tower itself, despite the recent collapse, remains the lair of a nest of four 6-foot-long bloodback centipedes, as well as a swarm of their smaller cousins. The vermin are extremely territorial, and they scuttle forth to attack anyone who pokes around in the rubble.

BLOODBACK CENTIPEDES (4)   CR 1/2
Medium monstrous centipede
hp 4 (MM 286)

CENTIPEDE SWARM   CR 4
hp 31 (MM 238)

D. The Crater

Although it's clearly visible from the sea, actually reaching the crater site by land is easier said than done. No trails lead to the site, and once one comes within a half mile of the actual crater, fallen trees and loose soil make travel even more exhausting. The terrain here is difficult, and overland travel speeds are reduced to one-quarter normal. Moving among the toppled and scorched trees makes for a strange and unnerving experience, since the only signs of life are the wheeling flocks of turkey vultures in the skies above. With the exception of akatas or void zombies, no wandering monster encounters occur here—treat encounters with other creatures as akata or zombie encounters.

Of course, the falling star was no natural event—it was called down to strike the ground above a specially prepared cavern adorned with strange magical glyphs placed there weeks ago by drow wizards working with ancient aboleth magic. As it was their first attempt using the complex glyphs, the drow made a few errors they hope to correct before they next call down a stone from the heavens above. First, they mistimed their calculations, and the meteor struck sooner than they anticipated, resulting in the deaths of a number of drow who were in the cavern below studying the glyphs. Second, the magic caused far too many localized events, such as the shadow in the sky above Riddleport, that gave away the fact that something strange was going on in the area. Finally, they brought down a chunk of rock covered in living—and extraordinarily dangerous—creatures, aliens in cocoon form. These creatures are known as akatas.

As a part of their bizarre physiology, the akatas clung to the outside of the meteor in noqual cocoons and rode it to the surface of Golarion. The extreme heat of atmospheric entry caused the akatas to awaken from their hibernation

---

NOQUAL

The metals found in fallen stars and on alien worlds are known collectively to Golarion's smiths and sages as "skymetal." The most common (yet still relatively rare in the grand scheme of ores) skymetal is adamantine, as this incredibly hard material survives the scouring touch of atmospheric entry with ease. Other variants of skymetal exist as well, although they are so rare that their properties are rumors to most.

Noqual is one such material, and it has arrived in relatively large amounts on the meteorite that struck Devil's Elbow. This strange metal looks almost like a pale green crystal to the untrained eye, but despite its appearance the stuff can be worked as iron. Noqual is light, half as heavy as iron, yet as strong as the same. More importantly, noqual is strangely resistant to magic. An object made of noqual gains a +4 bonus on any saving throw made against magical sources. Creating a magic item that incorporates any amount of noqual into it increases the price of creation by 5,000 gp, as costly reagents and alchemical supplies must be used to treat the metal during the process.

Weapons made of noqual weigh half as much as normal, and inflict +1 point of damage against constructs and undead created by feats or spells (this is an enhancement bonus to damage).

Armor made of noqual weighs half as much; noqual armor is one category lighter than normal for the purposes of movement and other limitations (light armor is still treated as light armor, though). The armor's maximum Dexterity bonus is increased by 2, and armor check penalties are lessened by 3. The armor's spell failure chance increases by 20% and applies to all magic cast while wearing the armor, regardless of the magic's source or class abilities possessed by the wearer. The wearer of a suit of noqual armor gains a +2 resistance bonus on all saving throws against spells and spell-like abilities.

Items without metal parts cannot be made from noqual. Noqual has 30 hit points per inch of thickness and hardness 10. Noqual ore is worth 50 gp per pound.

Type of Noqual Item	Item Cost Modifier
Light armor	+4,000 gp
Medium armor	+8,000 gp
Heavy armor	+12,000 gp
Shield	12,000 gp
Weapon or other items	+500 gp

---

within their exceedingly thick protective cocoons. Dozens of akatas survived the impact and hatched in the hours after the event. It took them several days to recover and acclimate to the island, but by the time the PCs arrive, the akatas have already had an impact on the environment.

When the drow priestess Shindiira sent scouts to investigate the crater, they discovered several newly freed akatas in the process of eating the remnants of their cocoons. When they attempted to capture some of the creatures, several drow were bitten and many more akatas were killed, but in the end the drow managed to catch quite a few and returned to their caves with them. These akatas have since perished to drow experiments. The drow also gathered up the remnants of the fallen star and all of the skymetal fragments they could find—there were no fragments too large to transport, and as a result, most of the evidence of the meteor itself is missing from the crater.

For each hour of searching the crater or the area within a thousand feet of its perimeter, a character has a 10% chance of finding a shard of pale green metal—a single pound of noqual, the type of skymetal the falling star brought to Golarion. Don't forget to check for wandering monsters while the PCs search—spending too many hours scrounging for noqual here more or less guarantees at least one run-in with akatas or void zombies. The most noqual that can be scavenged from the area is 15 pounds.

E. Zincher's Camp

Clegg Zincher initially chose Witchlight as his base of operations, but when he allied with the drow, he moved the site of his camp to this area. Two decrepit buildings, once homes for a pair of hunters, sit abandoned at the edge of the camp—these buildings are too close to collapse for Zincher's taste to use as a headquarters. This area is detailed in Part Four of the adventure.

F. Eastern Lighthouse (EL 5)

Although just as old as the other structures, this 40-foot-tall stone lighthouse survived the passage of time and the impact of the falling star quite well. Its walls are encrusted with salt and grime, and the wooden stairwell and internal floors have collapsed into a pile of moldering rubble within, but the tower itself stands firm.

Creature: It was from this tower that Yaris hurled himself after Virashi's death so many years ago. His suicide was also the death of Devil's Elbow as a civilized region, and heralded the mass exodus for other shores.

As a wraith, Yaris is powerless during the day. At these times, he hides in the walls of the stone tower, dormant and silent. At night, he emerges to scour the surrounding region, regret and fury at his poor decisions in life building his hate and wrath nightly and fueling his undead existence. He marks those who visit this place during the day, and if they remain on the island after dark, the vengeful wraith is sure to seek them out wherever they may be to murder them. The wraith made the mistake of attacking the drow only to be rebuked several times by their priestly leader, and now he suffers their existence here as long as they or their human allies do not approach within a mile of this tower.

YARIS NERAKEN   CR 5
Wraith
hp 32 (MM 258)

Treasure: Over the years, Yaris has murdered several adventurers who foolishly set foot on Devil's Elbow—the few wraiths that haunt the island after dark are his undead children (although he has little interest in controlling them and lets them wander as they will). The bodies of most of these fallen adventurers are long gone, but one of them remains in the tangled undergrowth on the southern side of this tower. The cliffside here has eroded dangerously close to the tower, and anyone who travels back here must make a DC 12 Balance check to avoid a slip over the edge (which results in a 70-foot fall to the rocky beach below for 7d6 points of damage). A DC 20 Search check is enough to notice the skeletal body—after dark, this check is automatic due to the soft blue glow of the magic blade visible through the roots and vines.

The body is that of a human dressed in rusted fragments of chain mail. Clutched in one skeletal hand is a *+1 cold iron longsword*; the sword's blade glows like a torch. At the skeleton's side is a rotted pouch and a small mound of 34 gp, 13 pp, and a single garnet worth 250 gp.

G. The Sea Caves

This area is detailed in Part Five of the Adventure.

PART THREE: WITCHLIGHT

The collection of crumbling buildings that once comprised the largest settlement on Devil's Elbow has long since fallen into disrepair, the recent impact having further damaged the buildings so that bits and pieces of the internal walls have collapsed. None of the buildings save the tower retain a complete roof. The stone-walled buildings themselves have weathered the passage of time rather well, and as a result made for an excellent campsite for the cyphermages.

Many years ago, when Devil's Elbow was the lair of the siren Virashi, this site was the haunt of a will-o'wisp that had allied itself to the siren. Although the malevolent creature was slain by adventurers, the will-o'wisp's haunt sometimes manifests in the region. The undead echo isn't powerful enough to physically harm anyone, and it has never directly confronted anyone as a result, but the periodic sightings of the ghostly lights were enough to earn the island yet another legend.

Today, Witchlight is abandoned and ruined. The only structure with a roof and solid footing remaining is the

Witchlight

1 square = 5 feet

old watchtower, the first and best-built structure on the entire island. Yet even it has suffered from the passage of time and the recent impact. When the cyphermages arrived in the region, they chose the tower as their base of operations. For the first day, it served them well, but now it has become a prison.

As detailed in the description of area **B5**, the last day has been particularly harrowing for the cyphermages—see the "Cyphermages in Witchlight" section for details on how the few surviving inhabitants of this area react to the PCs' approach.

B1. Unstable Buildings (EL 4)

A portion of the slate-covered roof of this stone house has collapsed into ruins—but the rest of the roof seems to be intact.

These stone houses once belonged to private citizens living in Witchlight.

Trap: Although portions of these buildings' roofs remain intact, this is more a fluke than any real testimony to architectural design. Inside, the walls creak and the roof sags dangerously, and pressure placed on the floorboards causes them to groan dramatically. As long as an intruder is relatively cautious and careful, he can explore this

otherwise empty room safely, but for each round combat or other violent activity takes place here, there's a flat 40% chance the building collapses. A collapse turns all of the terrain inside the building into difficult terrain.

COLLAPSING BUILDING   CR 4

Type mechanical; **Search** DC 15; **Disable Device** —

EFFECTS

Trigger proximity (40% chance/round); **Reset** none

Effect ceiling and walls collapse; multiple targets (all creatures inside building); 8d6 damage and knocked prone (Reflex DC 20 half damage and negates knockdown)

B2. Public Building

This building's rotting timbers still bear flecks of colorful paint, a sign that it must have looked grand in its heyday. Now it is little more than a collapsing ruin.

This served as Witchlight's sole government building—record hall, village jail, and a gathering hall for the settlement's residents. The structure has now almost completely fallen in on itself, the ceiling long gone.

Treasure: A DC 23 Search check of the building reveals an old silver comb set with strips of ivory that was accidentally left behind by the town's original inhabitants and is now partially buried under a collapsed wall. Because of its age and craftsmanship, the comb is worth 250 gp.

B3. Ruined Store (EL 4)

This large timber-and-stone structure stands at the edge of the steep southern slope, overlooking the sea far below. Large windows facing the village's main thoroughfare suggest a shop in at least one portion of the building, but the windows have been hastily boarded over. Several corpses lay near the outer walls of the building, obviously a source of interest for the circling turkey vultures above.

This combination of inn and store was the only two-story building in Witchlight, but now, while it's safe enough to navigate for at least a few more years, it's nearing the point of collapse. The corpses around the building consist of the four men Gravin Goldhammer sent up here yesterday to investigate the flashing lights. They were attacked by a pack of akatas before they managed to reach the tower, and their bodies now lay here, hosts to the akata larvae within. A DC 15 Survival check is enough to note that, while the bodies have attracted buzzards, the scavengers have not yet landed to feed, indicating something unusual is going on with the bodies. An investigation of the corpses determines that they were slain by numerous slashing blows and what appear to be bite marks. More horrifying, however, is the mutilated nature of their faces. Each body is missing its lower jaw; in its place is a nauseating, gray-green, twitching tendril that looks almost like a bloated tongue.

Creatures: The bloated "tongues" on the dead bodies are, in fact, portions of the akata larvae growing inside the corpses, and as soon as anyone approaches close enough to examine the bodies (or as soon as anyone attempts to destroy or move a body from afar), the larval akatas cause their undead hosts to rise up and attack. The undead are eerily silent—the only noise they make is the sound of their movements and a nasty muffled sloshing noise whenever their akata's tendril lashes out of their ruined faces to strike at a target.

VOID ZOMBIES (4)   CR 1
Variant human zombie (see page 81)
NE Medium undead
Init −1; **Senses** darkvision 60 ft.;
　　Listen +0, Spot +0

DEFENSE

AC 11, touch 9, flat-footed 1
　　(−1 Dex, +2 natural)
hp 16 each (2d12+3)
Fort +0, **Ref** −1, **Will** +3

Defensive Abilities undead traits; **DR** 5/slashing
Weaknesses vulnerable to critical hits

OFFENSE

Spd 30 ft.
Melee slam +2 (1d6+1) and
　　tongue −3 (1d4 plus blood drain)

TACTICS

During Combat Void zombies focus on the nearest foe and keep after them until they're dead or out of sight.
Morale Void zombies fight until destroyed.

STATISTICS

Str 12, **Dex** 8, **Con** —, **Int** —, **Wis** 10, **Cha** 1
Base Atk +1; **Grp** +2
Feats Toughness

SPECIAL ABILITIES

Blood Drain (Ex) If a void zombie hits a living creature with its tongue attack, it drains blood from the creature, inflicting 2 points of Strength damage before the tongue detaches.
Vulnerable to Critical Hits (Ex) Unlike most undead, void zombies are vulnerable to critical hits and sneak attacks. A critical hit to a void zombie indicates damage to the larval akata within its body.

B4. Watchtower Barracks

The reinforced windows, solid stone construction, and connection to a watchtower mark this building as a military structure of some kind.

When Witchlight acted as a small settlement, several guards barracked in this building, which also acted as a fortress of sorts during infrequent times of attack from pirates or the island's more dangerous inhabitants.

The outer door to the building was once solid oak, but it now hangs askew on its hinges; it collapses entirely if any attempt to open or close the door further is made. The rooms within the barracks are empty, but spattered with blood and signs of combat.

B5. Witchlight Watchtower

This fifty-foot-tall circular watchtower stands precariously on the edge of a steep slope overlooking the sea. The tower itself seems to be made of stone, yet no seams or individual blocks are apparent; it's as if the entire tower were formed from one block of stone. An enclosed octagonal platform protrudes from the tower roof.

The watchtower was the first structure created on Devil's Elbow, shaped from a *wall of stone* spell and reinforced from within with wooden supports and additional *stone shape* spells. The construction has served the structure well—until the falling star hit, the tower was solid and stable. Today, while the tower itself remains sound, the ground beneath it is not. The cliffside is crumbling, as should be evident to anyone who examines the soil around the area and makes a DC 20 Knowledge (architecture and engineering) check—unfortunately for the cyphermages within, none had this level of knowledge.

The door between area **B4** and **B5a** is closed and barred from the inside of area **B5a**. The portal itself is a heavy iron door. Knocking on it quickly rouses the attention of the cyphermages, if they aren't already expecting the PCs.

The interior floors of the tower are made of stone and reinforced with wooden timbers. The only furniture within consists of cots, a few tables, and other portable objects that were brought here by the cyphermages. Brief descriptions of the various chambers in the tower appear in the nearby sidebar.

The Cyphermages in Witchlight

Led by a wizard named Fenella Bromathan, the cyphermages arrived on Devil's Elbow 3 days before the PCs. Their first 2 days were relatively productive, although they were concerned that there didn't seem to be "enough noqual" around, considering the number of craters on the

---

WITCHLIGHT WATCHTOWER

Ceiling height inside the watchtower averages at 10 feet.

B5a. Ground Floor: This large open area is empty, save for a few mounds of destroyed furniture and other rubble.

B5b. Guardroom: One cyphermage is on guard here at all times.

B5c. Field Hospital: This room serves as a field hospital, with each bunk containing one badly wounded (0 hp) cyphermage. A DC 12 Search check reveals three healing kits stashed under the northern cot.

B5d. Barracks: The cyphermages who aren't mortally wounded take turns resting here, sleeping fitfully on bedrolls. A small chest kept here contains the noqual ore the cyphermages have recovered so far—three 1 pound lumps and one 6 pound block.

B5e. Storage Closets: These massive storage closets are empty.

B5f. Observation Room: From the observation platform on a clear day, a lookout can see for dozens of miles. The windows contain no glass, but can be closed with heavy, lockable wooden shutters.

---

island. Initially, the cyphermages assumed the shortage was because other prospectors had reached the sites before them, but now, the surviving cyphermages have come to suspect other reasons.

The original contingent of cyphermages numbered 12 in all; Fenella Bromathan, her new apprentice Samaritha Beldusk, and ten minor wizards who were along for the experience and to provide assistance. Of those 12, only five remain alive, and of those five, only three are conscious. Fenella was among the first to die the night the akatas converged on Witchlight and attacked the cyphermages. Faced with magic-resistant and deadly foes, the cyphermages were torn apart. Those who survived did so only by retreating to the watchtower and barricading themselves in. They could do little more than watch as the bodies of their dead, left in the rubble, eventually rose as void zombies and staggered off into the surrounding woodlands to seek out safe and secluded places to birth their alien young.

Since Fenella's death, Samaritha has assumed control of the operation. Periodically, she travels up to the top of the tower to fire off an eye-catching spell like *pyrotechnics* in hopes of attracting the attention of others on the island for help. When Goldhammer's men arrived late yesterday, the cyphermages thought they were rescued, but could only watch as the men refused to approach the ruins further without being met outside—a tactic that ended poorly for them as they were ambushed and slaughtered by akatas lurking in the nearby woods. When the cyphermages sighted the *Flying Cloud*, Samaritha did her best to attract the ship's attention with another *pyrotechnics* spell, and is now considering a risky flight down the mountainside to seek aid. Fear of the akatas and a sense of duty to the cyphermages too injured to move have kept her here for now.

When the PCs arrive in Witchlight, Samaritha is downstairs in area **B5c** of the tower, tending to the wounded with her two conscious wizards providing assistance—the cyphermages don't notice the PCs' arrival unless the characters are particularly loud. If combat breaks out in a nearby building, Samaritha quickly climbs up to the tower roof to throw open a window to see what's going on. If she sees the PCs, she says, "Stop there! Say something so I know you're alive." If one of the PCs is her favored companion, she calls that PC's name out in particular. In any event, she encourages all of the PCs to come to the tower immediately, warning them to be quick, since monsters have been lurking in the nearby woods.

Once the PCs are inside the tower with her, Samaritha leads them into area **B5d** to speak with them. She suspects that the akatas have noticed the PCs as well and might be massing for another attack, so she sends one of her cyphermages up top to area **B5f** to keep a watch before she bombards the PCs with questions, particularly asking them if they've encountered any of the "monsters" yet. She speaks, of course, of the akatas; she doesn't know what to call them, only that they're ferocious, resistant to magic, probably venomous, and that those whom the creatures kill arise as zombies. She breathlessly and quickly recounts the story of her time on the island, and ends by practically begging the PCs to heal her injured companions and then lead them off the island to safety.

Samaritha and her companions are all wounded to one degree or another, but she's quick to point out that none of them have been bitten by the monsters—an important distinction, she says, since those who were bitten and then later died rose as zombies. She points to the void zombies as an example if she saw the PCs fighting against them. Unless the PCs come up with a much better plan, Samaritha

wants to remain holed up here in the relative safety of the tower until a ship arrives, at which point she's willing to risk the journey downhill to rescue (provided the PCs are there to help protect her and her fellow wizards).

If the PCs ask Samaritha or the other cyphermages about drow sightings on the island, they shake their heads—they've seen no dark elves during their time here.

Of course, no matter what the PCs decide to do, things change quickly when the akatas move in to lay siege to the tower one last time.

SAMARITHA BELDUSK — CR 4

Female half-elf transmuter 4

CG Medium humanoid (elf)

Init +1; **Senses** low-light vision; Listen +3, Spot +3 (+6 in shadows)

DEFENSE

AC 16, touch 12, flat-footed 15

(+4 armor, +1 deflection, +1 Dex)

hp 15 (currently 10; HD 4d4+4)

Fort +2, **Ref** +2, **Will** +4; +2 against enchantment

Immune sleep

OFFENSE

Spd 30 ft.

Melee mwk dagger +2 (1d4–1/19–20)

Ranged mwk dagger +4 (1d4–1/19–20)

Spell-Like Ability (CL 4th)

1/day—*mage hand*

Spells Prepared (CL 4th; CL 5th with transmutation; +3 ranged touch)

2nd—*levitate, pyrotechnics* (2, DC 16), *scorching ray*

1st—*feather fall, mage armor, magic missile* (2), *ray of enfeeblement*

0—*light* (4)

Prohibited Schools abjuration, illusion

TACTICS

Before Combat Samaritha has taken to casting *pyrotechnics* at dusk in an attempt to attract the attention of others on the island; she also may have cast one already in an attempt to signal the *Flying Cloud*. She casts *mage armor* as soon as she feels that combat is about to begin.

During Combat Samaritha starts most combats by levitating and then relying heavily on her ranged spells and wands to attack foes on the ground.

Morale Samaritha won't abandon her cyphermages, and

Samaritha
Beldusk

fights to the death to protect them or any other friends and allies. Left to her own devices, she flees combat if brought below 5 hit points.

STATISTICS

Str 8, **Dex** 12, **Con** 13, **Int** 16, **Wis** 10, **Cha** 14

Base Atk +2; **Grp** +1

Feats Alertness (as long as Leniloria is in arm's reach), Scribe Scroll, Spell Focus (transmutation), Varisian Tattoo (transmutation)

Skills Concentration +8, Decipher Script +10, Diplomacy +4, Gather Information +4, Knowledge (arcana) +10, Knowledge (local) +4, Listen +3, Search +4, Spellcraft +12, Spot +3 (+6 in shadows)

Languages Common, Elven, Halfling, Varisian

SQ summon familiar (owl named Leniloria)

Combat Gear *wand of magic missile* (18 charges), *wand of identify* (37 charges); **Other Gear** *bracers of armor +1*, masterwork dagger, *ring of protection +1*, belt pouch, black enameled writing set worth 25 gp, silk rope (50 ft.), abacus worth 15 gp, magnifying glass, flint and tinder, 34 gp; **Spellbook** contains all cantrips and prepared spells plus: 1st—*animate rope, reduce person*; 2nd—*daze monster*

SPECIAL ABILITIES

Varisian Tattoo This feat, detailed in the *Pathfinder Chronicles Campaign Setting*, grants Samaritha *mage hand* once per day as a spell-like ability and increases her effective caster level for transmutation spells by one.

CYPHERMAGE (4)   CR 1

Human wizard 1

N Medium humanoid

Init +2; **Senses** Listen +1, Spot +1

DEFENSE

AC 16, touch 12, flat-footed 4
(+4 armor, +2 Dex)

hp 5 each (two currently at 2, two currently at 0; HD 1d4+1)

Fort +1, **Ref** +2, **Will** +3

OFFENSE

Spd 30 ft.

Melee mwk dagger +1 (1d4/19–20)

Ranged mwk dagger +3 (1d4/19–20)

Spells Prepared (CL 1st)
1st—*mage armor, magic missile*
0—*light* (3)

TACTICS

During Combat cyphermages are scholars and readers, and the concept of battle leaves most of them quaking in their boots. They cast *mage armor* as soon as possible, then *magic missile* at the closest foe.

Morale Once a Cyphermage has cast *magic missile* or is wounded, he flees to somewhere safe.

STATISTICS

Str 10, **Dex** 14, **Con** 13, **Int** 15, **Wis** 12, **Cha** 8

Base Atk +0; **Grp** +0

Feats Combat Casting, Scribe Scroll, Skill Focus (Decipher Script)

Skills Concentration +5, Decipher Script +9, Knowledge (arcana) +6, Knowledge (local) +6, Spellcraft +6

Languages Common, Elven, Varisian

SQ summon familiar (none currently)

Gear mwk dagger, robes, several sheets of parchment and writing instruments, 10 sp; **Spellbook** contains all cantrips and all spells prepared

The Akata Siege (EL 6)

Time this encounter so that it begins at some point when the majority (preferably all) of the PCs are in the Witchlight Watchtower. When their conversation with Samaritha seems to be winding down, or the PCs seem ready to leave the tower, the cyphermage guard atop the tower cries out an alarm: "Here they come again!" Samaritha's face grows pale with fear and she races downstairs to make sure that the door to area B4 is closed tightly, telling the PCs that the monsters have often launched attacks on the tower after anyone spends a significant amount of time wandering around outside. She's not sure why the creatures didn't attack the PCs earlier, but suspects that their activity cycles might have something to do with it.

Characters who open a window or climb up to area B5f can watch as the akatas surge out of the surrounding forest. The alien monsters are unnaturally silent as they move, and shockingly fast and limber, their bodies moving with a strangely nauseating grace as they gallop into the ruins. Some of the creatures stop to paw at any bodies or pieces of gear left outside; if any living creature is outside at this time, four akatas break off to attack that target. In all, two dozen of the horrific creatures participate in the attack, more than twice the number seen in previous assaults. The cyphermages respond to this unexpected increase in the number of akatas with shock—but Samaritha admits she feared their numbers were growing.

As the wave of akatas reaches the tower, the beasts begin scrambling up the sides and scratching at its foundations. Play up the unsettling noises the PCs hear and how it sounds like the entire place is crawling with the mysterious monsters (which it is). The creatures hammer and claw and bite at the tower's windows and door—make it clear that the window shutters won't hold forever, although they seem fairly strong for the moment. You can add tension to this encounter by having the locked shutters of a window near one of the PCs partially shatter, allowing the akata beyond to try to strike at a nearby foe with its tentacles.

Eventually, at some place in the tower you choose, one of those windows breaks completely. The windows aren't

large enough for akatas to clamber through easily—they need to make a DC 20 Escape Artist check to slither into the tower, a requirement that should limit the rate at which the monsters can infiltrate the tower. The broken window should be near at least one PC, who immediately becomes the akata's target.

One round after this combat begins, a tremor shakes the entire tower. All creatures (akatas included) standing in the tower must make a DC 10 Balance check or fall prone. The tremor lasts only a few seconds, but afterward the tower has a barely perceptible lean to the south. The sudden weight of all the dense-bodied akatas is finishing the job the meteor began—the weakened cliffside under the watchtower's foundations is about to give way.

A few rounds later (roll 1d4 to determine the number, or simply pick one that adds to the drama as you see fit), a second tremor shakes the tower. It quickly becomes apparent that this tremor is much more significant. Every creature in the tower must make a DC 15 Balance check to keep its footing as the tower sags to the southwest. A terrible noise like endless thunder grows louder by the moment.

The next round, the ground gives way. The stone tower topples over onto its side, throwing every creature against the (now horizontal) western wall. All creatures in the tower must make a DC 10 Reflex save to avoid taking 1d6 points of falling damage—for each floor a creature is higher than the ground floor, the damage taken increases by 1d6 and the save DC increases by 1. For example, characters in area **B5f** when the tower falls must make a DC 13 save to avoid taking 4d6 points of damage.

The round after the tower falls, it begins rolling down the steep slope toward the waters of the lagoon below. Immense cracks begin radiating up along the sides of the tower as it follows a landslide of rock and rubble downward. Any characters inside the tower are carried along for a harrowing ride, but the tower's shape serves to help slow the fall somewhat. Akatas clinging to the side of the tower scramble for purchase—some tumble away to join the rocks and dirt on the fall into the sea below, while others cling to the outside of the tower only to be crushed as it rolls over onto them. Any creature within 10 feet of the outside of the tower when it falls must make a DC 15 Reflex save to avoid being swept away by the landslide as well; those who make this save remain on top of the ridge, while those who fail are carried along by the landslide. Treat the landslide as an avalanche (DMG 90) for those who aren't sheltered by virtue of being inside the tower when it collapses.

Those inside the tower aren't completely protected. It takes the tower 3 rounds to roll all the way down the side of the ridge and splash into the water below. At the same time, a few akatas manage to get inside the tower, either through torn-open windows or via the increasing number of large holes appearing in the tower's magically constructed walls as it continues its violent descent.

The best way to run these 3 rounds is not as a full combat on a battlemap. Instead, have each PC, NPC, and akata roll for Initiative as normal. Each round, all creatures can make one of three choices on their turn as to how they wish to account for the rolling motion of the tower.

Brace: As a move-equivalent action, a creature can attempt to brace itself in a stairwell, doorway, crack in a wall, or support timber by making a DC 15 Climb check. Succeeding at the Climb check by 5 or more allows the creature to brace itself with one hand free. A braced creature takes no damage from the rolling of the tower. A creature that braced itself during a previous round gains a +4 circumstance bonus on this Climb check.

Ride: A creature can attempt to ride along with the tower, moving and jumping along with the rolling motion to prevent itself from being battered. Riding the tower requires a move action and either a DC 15 Balance check (if the creature isn't trying to move to a particular area) or a DC 15 Tumble check (if the creature is attempting to end up next to a specific target). Akatas make Tumble checks to attack PCs on their turns.

Escape: A creature can attempt to escape the tower entirely if it's adjacent to an open window, door, or hole in a wall by making a DC 15 Jump check as a move action. Success indicates that it leaps free of the tower, but unless it can fly, it is immediately swept up by the surrounding landslide. With a DC 15 Reflex save, the escaping creature grabs a dangling root or a solid ledge of rock and halts its fall, but otherwise it is carried down to the bottom of the slope by the landslide.

Rolling Events: On each creature's turn, roll 1d20 to determine how the tower's rolling impacts that character and determines what type of actions he can take on his turn.

1d20	Rolling Event
1–5	**Smooth Rolling:** No unusual situations occur for that character. He may attempt to ride, but not to escape. There's a 50% chance something solid enough nearby gives him the opportunity to attempt to brace.
6–10	**Visitor:** A non-braced character passes within 5 feet of the current character. Determine which other character

THE TUMBLING TOWER

The following rules should help you adjudicate situations that may arise during the tower's 3-round tumble into the sea.

Magic: Spells such as *fly*, *levitation*, *meld into stone*, and *spider climb* allow a character to brace or ride automatically. Such a character can leave both hands free if he chooses in order to attack or cast spells. *Feather fall* grants a character a +20 circumstance bonus on Tumble or Balance checks made to ride. Spells such as *entangle* and *web* cast outside the tower slow the tower's descent so that it takes 5 rounds to reach the bottom, but grants everyone within a +4 circumstance bonus on attempts to brace or ride. Alternatively, a *web* spell cast inside the tower automatically braces any creatures caught in the area. A hasted character gains a +20 haste bonus on any attempt to brace or ride, while a slowed character takes a −20 penalty on such checks.

Spellcasting. The rolling tower constitutes extraordinarily violent motion—spellcasting in the tower requires a DC 20 Concentration check. A flying creature with at least good maneuverability that chooses to ride is not considered to be under violent motion and need not make this check.

Jostled: A character who fails to brace, ride, or escape (or a character who chooses to do nothing) becomes jostled by the tower and takes 2d6 points of damage each round (DC 15 Reflex for half) and is knocked prone. Unconscious characters are automatically considered jostled.

passes randomly from all other PCs, NPCs, and akatas in the area (braced characters do not count for this check). A PC can attempt to grab a tumbling PC or NPC by making a melee touch attack and making a DC 14 Strength check—doing so grants the grabbed character a +4 bonus on checks made to brace, ride, or escape. If the visitor is an akata, the character can attack it. (This is the only result on an akata's turn that allows it to attack a PC.)

11–13	**Small Crack:** If the character is braced, a crack opens in the wall nearby; if the character is not braced, the crack passes within 5 feet of his position. A character may attempt to escape through a small crack.
14	**Large Crack:** As "small crack" above, save that the hole is large enough that the character might fall out of it. Attempts to escape are automatically successful. A character who's not trying to escape must make a DC 12 Reflex save to avoid falling out of the hole anyway.
15	**Debris:** As "smooth rolling" above, save that a blast of dust and pebbles strikes the character in the face—he must make a DC 12 Fortitude save to avoid being blinded for 1 round. A blind character cannot ride or escape, and can only brace if he braced the previous round.

16–20 Solid Object: A character who is already bracing can automatically brace this round. A character who did not brace the last round can attempt to brace this round.

AKATAS (24)   CR 1
hp 11 each (see page 80)

Development: At the bottom of the slope, the tower plunges into the sea. The impact is softened by the water, and characters within the tower are automatically knocked prone unless they were bracing on the previous round. The impact also inflicts a final 2d6 points of damage to everyone (Reflex DC 15 halves). The tower's magical construction prevented it from completely collapsing, but enough holes exist now that the waves swiftly rush in—likewise, the PCs should have little problem clambering out of the tower and onto the beach. The water here isn't deep enough to completely submerge the fallen tower, but it is enough to damage the akatas, as the salt water acts as an extremely powerful acid on those creatures. Any surviving and conscious akatas thrash in freakishly silent agony as the salt water eats away at them, dealing 4d6 points of damage per round. The water should slay any surviving akatas from the assault with relative ease.

While Samaritha uses *feather fall* to greatly increase the likelihood of her own survival, the collapsing tower is quite likely to kill the other cyphermages. The PCs can attempt to save them as best they can during the fall, of course. In any event, any surviving cyphermages (Samaritha included) quickly realize that their shelter is gone. Desperate and afraid, they look to the PCs for direction on where to go next. Left to their own devices, Samaritha would use *levitate* to ferry the survivors back up to the ridge above. The cyphermages then make their way to Zincher's camp to beg for help. Without levitation or flight, the climb back up to the top is difficult but not impossible—it's a DC 15 Climb check to scale the cliffs, but only a DC 10 Climb check to scramble up the slope in the landslide's wake. Few beaches surround the base of the island's cliffs, so walking the perimeter isn't really an option—swimming, however, is (although feel free to hit swimming parties with a few encounters with sharks, reefclaws, or other aquatic menaces). Note that characters who swim to the east have a good chance of accidentally stumbling across the drow caves (see Part Five).

Ad Hoc XP Award: Award the PCs experience points as if they had defeated a CR 6 creature for surviving this harrowing encounter. For each Cyphermage who survives the fall, award the PCs additional XP as if they had defeated that Cyphermage in combat.

PART FOUR: ZINCHER'S CAMP

When the falling star struck Devil's Elbow, many saw it as an ill omen, while others saw it as an opportunity for cash. Clegg Zincher, alone among Riddleport's prospectors and doomsayers, saw the falling star as something more. He immediately thought of the legend of Earthfall as he watched the falling star and its explosion safely from the balcony of his home. Certainly, the prospect that the stone brought skymetal was enticing enough, but what if this stone was akin to the *Starstone* itself? What untold strength could be gained by the first person to find the stone and harness its power?

Within hours of the meteor's strike, while the rest of Riddleport reeled in the aftermath of the event, Zincher was already working to bring together a crew of men with strong backs and weak minds. Zincher even called in his favorite knee-breaker and thug-wrangler, a Garundi mercenary whose skills he had used many times before—a man named Akron Erix.

It took longer than Zincher wanted to actually make it to Devil's Elbow, but he was pleasantly surprised to find upon arrival that his first competitors, thugs in the employ of rival crimelord Avery Slyeg, were nowhere to be seen. Assuming they had fallen victim to local wildlife, Zincher ordered many of his men to steal Slyeg's ship and sail it to Roderic's Cove for safekeeping while he, Erix, and the rest of his thugs moved to Witchlight to set up a camp. Along the way, Zincher's men uncovered their first fragments of noqual. As the expedition moved closer to the impact crater, it found larger chunks of the rare ore, but it also came under attack from the invading akatas and lost several men to the strange monsters before defeating them.

Where most of his men saw only death and terror, Zincher saw opportunity. The strange and horrible monsters could make excellent additions to his arena back in Riddleport, and if a method for breeding them could be devised, they could even become a new commodity under Zincher's control. He ordered the construction of several dozen cages, hoping to catch some of the monsters. Zincher assumed that the monsters were the fate that befell Slyeg's men, but that night he learned the truth when his camp was invaded by the drow.

This group of drow now knew better what to expect of intruders after interrogating some of Slyeg's men before they expired. Shindiira had her drow hold back in reserve, and slid unnoticed into Zincher's tent to confront the man on her own. Staggered and dumbfounded at the arrival of a dark elf in his camp, Zincher was an easy target for Shindiira's *scroll of charm monster*. Once enraptured by the beautiful priestess, Zincher agreed to serve as the aboveground guardian and custodian of the island while the drow finished their work below.

The next morning, Zincher relocated his camp to a point closer to the hidden path leading to the drow cave so that he could better guard that approach. He gave his men no explanation for the move, and ever since, they have remained at the campsite near two partially collapsed buildings on the eastern side of the island. Zincher's thugs spend their days scouring the island for deposits of noqual, and their nights huddled in their tents. They fear the akatas and the strange zombies that seem to be increasing in number on the island, but more so they fear Zincher and his unusual moods of late.

Clegg and his men can be found at area **E** on Devil's Elbow. The NPCs of note are described below, as is the campsite itself. For details on Clegg's reaction to the PCs, see "An Audience with Clegg" on page 35.

Clegg Zincher

Clegg Zincher is one of Riddleport's more publicly known, respected, and feared crimelords. Although his primary sources of income are from the city's arena and various semi-legal (and outright illegal) activites involving groups of unskilled laborers, he meddles in numerous affairs all across Riddleport. While his influence over the city continues to rise, the amount of control he can exert directly remains frustratingly low—at least, to him it does.

Now that Zincher has fallen under the influence of the drow, his paranoia has grown. The magic makes him see

the drow as allies, but he fears that if such an allegiance were to be made public, his reputation would be ruined. Gone are his initial plans to harvest skymetal, capture new creatures for his arena, or even his hopes that the falling star would transform him into a god. Now, Zincher's only real goal is to leave Devil's Elbow with his reputation and skin intact. He continues to send his men out to scout for akatas and search for skymetal, but takes little interest in their successes. He waits with growing worry and impatience for the drow to leave the island, thereby allowing him the chance to leave, and has taken increasingly to public whippings and beatings of men whom he suspects complain about the extended length of the stay here. As long as the drow remain, Zincher sees no easy route for escape.

Clegg Zincher is a broad-shouldered man. He has short gray hair and the leathery, wrinkled face of a man who spent most of his youth working under the sun. His beard is short and stubbly, almost an afterthought, and he wears at all times an *amulet of natural armor +1* bearing an image of a two-headed roc (few know that the amulet is all Zincher has to remember his father, a man he respected and feared until his death at sea). Zincher wears a leather cord on one shoulder, on which he has threaded several dried goblin ears—trophies from his first triumphant battle. Predatory flightless birds fascinate Zincher. They often serve in his arena as mascots (never as combatants), and he's brought along a trio of trained axebeaks on this trip to serve him as guardians and companions.

CLEGG ZINCHER   CR 8

Male human expert 2/rogue 7

CN Medium humanoid

Init +1; **Senses** Listen +6, Spot +6

DEFENSE

AC 18, touch 14, flat-footed 17
   (+3 armor, +3 deflection, +1 Dex, +1 natural)

hp 52 (9d6+18)

Fort +6, **Ref** +6, **Will** +4

Defensive Abilities evasion, trap sense +2, uncanny dodge

OFFENSE

Spd 30 ft.

Melee mwk pickaxe +12/+7 (1d8+6/×4)

Ranged mwk throwing axe +8/+3 (1d6+4)

Special Attacks sneak attack +4d6

TACTICS

Before Combat Zincher drinks his *potion of shield of faith +3* as soon as it becomes apparent that a fight against more than one opponent is about to break out.

During Combat Zincher prefers to fight with his axebeaks at his side, trusting them to prevent his enemies from surrounding him. In battle, he loudly yells profanities and

PICKAXE

A two-handed version of the heavy pick, the brutal pickaxe is equally effective at breaking up earth and stone as it is at sundering flesh and bone. Often a weapon of convenience for commoners, the pickaxe is also a favorite among brutes and thugs who value the intimidation factor afforded by the immense weapon.

Pickaxe: Cost 14 gp; Dmg (S) 1d6; Dmg (L) 1d8; Critical ×4; Weight 12 lb.; Type Piercing

curses at his foes, attempting to intimidate them while attacking them with his pickaxe. Zincher has murdered many with his trusty axe, but only the murders of note warrant notches on its handle.

Morale Normally, Zincher would flee if reduced to less than 15 hit points, but the charm affecting him prevents him from doing so if he fears that would place his drow mistress in peril of being discovered.

STATISTICS

Str 18, **Dex** 12, **Con** 14, **Int** 10, **Wis** 8, **Cha** 14

Base Atk +6; **Grp** +9

Feats Combat Reflexes, Great Fortitude, Persuasive, Quick Draw, Weapon Focus (pick axe)

Skills Bluff +14, Diplomacy +6, Forgery +12, Handle Animal +7, Intimidate +16, Jump +18, Knowledge (local) +12, Listen +6, Sense Motive +11, Spot +6, Tumble +10

Languages Common

SQ trapfinding

Combat Gear *potion of cure moderate wounds* (2), *potion of shield of faith +3*, acid (2), alchemist's fire (20); **Other Gear** *+1 leather armor*, masterwork pickaxe, masterwork throwing axes (4), dagger, *amulet of natural armor +1*, *gauntlets of ogre power*, lantern, 20 feet of silk rope, collection of goblin ear trophies, key to lockbox in area **E5** and the chest in **E6**, 24 pp

Akron Erix

Although he frequently works for Clegg Zincher during his numerous and extended visits to Riddleport, Akron Erix's loyalty is to his current contract first. He holds a well-deserved reputation for his agility in battle and dedication to his mission. Although this latter trait generally only applies to jobs as long as the coin lasts, it also means he holds his employers' secrets safe and he never reveals for whom he works. Unfortunately for Zincher, his current contract is not the one Erix signed with Zincher himself, but rather with the Sable Company of Korvosa.

The Sable Company is a group of specially trained marines from Korvosa who occasionally preemptively strike at the city's foes. Just over 4 years ago, Zincher sniffed out the Sable Company's previous spy and informant in Riddleport and delivered the agent's unspeakably mutilated corpse to the middle of Korvosa's largest market. Unwilling to let Riddleport go unwatched, the Sable Company recruited Akron Erix to take on the job. For his service, the Company promised Erix not only a payment of gold, but also that they'd put in a good word with the Order of the Fire Ghost, a sect of monks to which Erix once belonged. After his temper resulted in the crippling of a fellow monk, Erix was banished from the order, and ever since he's been working at reigning in his temper and trying to earn a way back into the order's good graces. Erix has been in and out of Riddleport dozens of times in the past 4 years, but his recent stint with Zincher has lasted the longest. Rumors that ill times have come to Korvosa worry Akron, and he hopes to be able to return there soon to report what he's learned of Zincher's operations in Varisia over the past 10 months.

A towering yet graceful dark-skinned man with a soft voice and a love of cheap cigars, Akron Erix rarely wears anything other than loose trousers, bracers, and thick-soled knee-high boots. He carries himself with the confidence of an experienced pugilist and someone unafraid of breaking knees, necks, or spines. When the PCs first arrive at Zincher's camp, Akron is unfriendly, both because his job requires him to be suspicious of people and because, although he knows of the PCs' reputation, he can't dare trust them.

Akron hasn't seen any drow on the island, but if he's told about Depora (or if he already knew of her as a result of a public battle between the PCs and the drow at the end of the previous adventure) and her links here, he grows thoughtful and admits that Zincher's been acting funny lately, like he's got a secret. Akron asks Zincher about the drow the next chance he gets; if he sees through Zincher's bluff, he'll return to the PCs and confirm to them that Zincher may know more about the dark elves, and then decides it's time to reveal his true nature. After telling the PCs about his real mission here, he asks them to help him capture Zincher alive so they can interrogate him about the drow and prepare for his deportation to Korvosa, where he's wanted on several charges of piracy, smuggling, and even a few murders from visits to the city years ago.

AKRON ERIX   CR 6

Male human ex-monk 2/fighter 4

N Medium humanoid

Init +6; **Senses** Listen +7, Spot +7

DEFENSE

AC 15, touch 15, flat-footed 13

(+1 deflection, +2 Dex, +2 Wis)

hp 40 (6 HD; 2d8+4d10+6)

Fort +8, **Ref** +6, **Will** +6

Defensive Abilities evasion

OFFENSE

Spd 30 ft.

Melee +1 cold iron warhammer +10/+5 (1d8+6/×3) or
unarmed strike +9/+4 (1d6+2) or
flurry of blows +7/+7/+2 (1d6+2)

TACTICS

During Combat In order to keep his cover intact, Akron fights against the PCs if and when combat breaks out, although he uses full defense actions combined with disarm attempts in order to show the PCs he doesn't want to kill any of them.

Morale Once it becomes clear the PCs have the upper hand against Zincher's men, Akron reveals himself as an agent of Korvosa and attempts to stun and capture Zincher rather than kill him. If the PCs use deadly force against him and bring him down to half his hit points or less, he withdraws from combat completely, taking his chances with the road back to Witchlight and the docks to await the arrival of a ship.

STATISTICS

Str 15, **Dex** 14, **Con** 12, **Int** 10, **Wis** 14, **Cha** 8

Base Atk +6; **Grp** +8

Feats Combat Reflexes, Deflect Arrows, Improved Grapple, Improved Initiative, Lightning Reflexes, Weapon Focus (unarmed strike, warhammer), Weapon Specialization (unarmed strike, warhammer)

Skills Intimidate +7, Jump +13, Listen +7, Sense Motive +7, Spot +7, Tumble +9

Languages Common

Combat Gear potion of barkskin +3, potion of lesser restoration; **Other Gear** +1 cold iron warhammer, ring of protection +1, five fine Chelish cigars worth 5 gp each, key to lockbox in area **E5**, 46 pp

Zincher's Thugs

Zincher arrived on Devil's Elbow with 60 thugs, by far the largest group of prospectors. He sent 40 of these men with his ship and the captured *Black Bunyip* to Roderic's Cove, and in the days that followed, 10 of his remaining men were killed by akatas, void zombies, accidents, or other perils on the island. The remaining 10 thugs are desperate, but still not quite desperate enough to openly oppose Zincher or his man Erix.

None of the thugs know anything about the drow on the island, but mentioning to them that there may be dark elves as

well on Devil's Elbow is enough to spook them and grant a +2 circumstance bonus on any future Intimidate checks made against them here on the island.

ZINCHER THUGS (10)   CR 1/2

Human warrior 1

NE Medium humanoid

Init +0; **Senses** Listen +0, Spot +0

DEFENSE

AC 13, touch 10, flat-footed 13
(+3 armor)

hp 5 (1d8+1)

Fort +3, **Ref** +0, **Will** +0

OFFENSE

Spd 30 ft.

Melee short sword +3 (1d6+1/19–20) or
unarmed strike +2 (1d3+1)

Ranged shortbow +1 (1d6/×3)

TACTICS

During Combat Zincher's thugs enjoy getting into scraps and eagerly jump into a fight against the PCs, seeing the chance to fight "actual men and women" as a welcome break from fights against monsters. They make a lot of noise when fighting, regardless of their true effectiveness.

Morale Once a thug takes any damage at all, he switches to a fully defensive stance and tries to back out of combat. If more than half of a particular group of thugs is dropped or driven off, the remaining half have a 50% chance of surrendering and a 50% of fighting to the death in desperation (roll separately for each thug).

STATISTICS

Str 13, **Dex** 11, **Con** 12, **Int** 9, **Wis** 10, **Cha** 8

Base Atk +1; **Grp** +2

Feats Improved Unarmed Strike, Weapon Focus (short sword)

Skills Intimidate +3

Languages Common

Gear studded leather armor, short sword, shortbow with 20 arrows, 10 gp

The Camp

The plume of smoke from Zincher's camp can be seen from anywhere on the island during the day. At night, the glow from the bonfire itself is visible within a half-mile of the camp. The entire camp stands in a wide forest

Akron Erix

clearing just off the western side of the trail and about 200 feet south of two partially collapsed buildings. One massive tent dominates this encampment, with three lesser olive-green tents to the south and a line of relatively small canvas tents along the north end. Ahead of the massive tent and between the lines of the others slowly burns a huge bonfire, creating a tremendous plume of white smoke. Sections of high palisade walls offer minimal protection around the edges of the camp, although stacked tree trunks and lines of narrow, deep trenches indicate the palisade is meant to eventually engulf the entire camp.

Of the 20 men and women who remained with Zincher and Erix on Devil's Elbow, 10 still live. Of those, two are within hours of void death when the PCs arrive. Initially, the 20 thugs bickered and fought over the limited bedspace in the camp, but now they have trouble sleeping when they're the only one in a tent at a time. At any one time during the day, four guards led by Erix scout the surrounding forest for noqual deposits or akatas to catch while the remaining four stay here, patrolling the grounds. Dinner takes place at nightfall, after which most of the guards gather around the bonfire to boast or play cards. By 2 hours after nightfall, the majority of the guards are asleep, although each pulls a guard shift during the night—there are always two guards posted near the bonfire. If the guards spot the PCs, they call out greetings and instruct the PCs to stay where they are until they can be escorted into camp. Less than a minute later, the wandering pair of guards arrives and brings the PCs into the camp from the east side, leading them into the large open space surrounded by tents and containing the massive bonfire.

When the PCs first arrive, Zincher's thugs are unfriendly. Diplomacy has no chance of improving their attitude above unfriendly, since the thugs have no time for "pretty talk." The use of Intimidate, however, they understand, and it can improve their attitude. In any event, the guards are quick to call on Zincher to meet the PCs.

E1. Bonfire

Puffing out a massive column of white smoke, this large bonfire slowly burns the tall pile of wet boughs and branches piled up here. The wood gives off a pleasant aroma as it crackles and pops.

The major task for those thugs neither on guard duty nor sleeping is to bring in firewood for the bonfire and to make sure it stays lit. To that end, two woodpiles nearby are constantly added to by thugs returning from the forest throughout the day (but not at night).

E2. Sleeping Tents

A small cooking-fire pit sits in front of each four-man tent, a tripod of sticks holding a pot above the barely glowing coals.

Each one of these tents is large enough for up to four humans to sleep rather snugly in the pair of two-person bunk beds within. Instead of cots, the thugs sleep on tough leather hides to insulate them and their bedrolls from the cold, hard ground. In addition to the sleeping thugs, each tent also contains additional bedrolls, bags of clothing and personal effects, and the weapons of any sleeping thugs.

During the evening, three of these tents contain two sleeping thugs apiece, with the remaining two standing guard outside at the bonfire. All of the tents are empty during daytime hours.

E3. Infirmary Tent (EL 2)

The entrance flap to this tent is stitched shut. Any thug that sees a PC attempting to enter this tent confronts the PC, informing them that the contents of the tent are "off limits." A thug calls Zincher if the PCs ignore the command—Zincher isn't interested in letting the PCs see what's inside the tent, and if he has to, he uses force to prevent the PCs from gaining access to the tent.

Four cots sit inside this tent, with a stump in the center of the tent acting as an impromptu table. On the stump burn several candles, most of which have nearly melted down to stubs.

Creatures: Inside this tent lie two of Zincher's men. Both are in the advanced stages of void death—Zincher's keeping them here in the hopes of harvesting the larval akatas, theorizing that they'll be easier to transport if he can figure a way to get them out of their zombie hosts without killing them. He's tried to do so twice before, but failed each time. Both men are strapped tightly into their cots.

If the men aren't healed within 6 hours of the PCs' first arrival in the camp, they transform into void zombies and begin thrashing violently. Zincher and Erix attempt to remove the larval akatas from these zombies, but are destined to fail again. The grisly work disgusts Erix, and if he makes peaceful contact with the PCs before the transformation, he might quietly recruit the PCs to heal the men of their affliction, letting them into the tent secretly. If Zincher realizes the men have been cured, he flies into a rage and attacks the PCs unless they can soothe his sudden hostility with words or magic.

VOID ZOMBIES (2)   **CR 1**
hp 16 each (see page 22)

E4. Supply Tent

The flap of this olive-green tent is unsecured and waves gently in the breeze. Occasionally, its motion reveals an interior filled with crates, barrels, bags, and boxes, lit by a flickering light.

All of the camp's food supplies and equipment are stored in this tent. A dozen small crates, four small barrels, two dozen bags, and a score of boxes fill this tent. The boxes and bags contain foodstuffs the thugs have been augmenting with game they've killed on the island. Two of the barrels are emptied ale kegs filled with fresh water from a nearby stream, and the other two still contain cheap ale. Inside the crates are tools (shovels, pickaxes, saws, hammers, and the like), extra bedrolls and tents (those of the now-dead thugs), coils of rope, candles and torches, and other mundane supplies.

E5. Akron Erix's Tent (EL 5)

This large, olive-green tent is relatively empty, containing only a single cot, a large leather bag, and a small metal lockbox.

A minimalist in his living as well as his dress, Akron keeps his tent almost completely empty. The large bag contains various clothes and several wooden boxes of cheap Korvosan cigars. Akron is only in his tent for 7 hours each day, from roughly 10:00 in the morning to about 5:00 in the afternoon.

Treasure: The small lockbox contains the payroll for this operation. An exceptional lock (DC 30 Open Lock) protects the box's contents—both Akron and Clegg carry keys for the box.

Inside the box is a list of 60 names (the original number of thugs Zincher brought to the island) folded in half and set on top of several small leather bags that contain a total of 200 sp, 200 gp, and 20 pp.

E6. Zincher's Pavilion

This immense red pavilion sticks out in the forest setting. Easily fifteen feet tall and twenty feet wide, the tent is larger than many buildings in Riddleport.

This is Zincher's home away from Riddleport. Usually, he brings with him all manner of amenities. This trip, however, has run into numerous unforeseen complications (namely, the akatas) which drastically reduced the number of good strong backs to carry his things. Despite having to "rough it," Zincher still occupies a lavish tent. Unlike the other tents, Zincher's pavilion has its own flooring (made of leather-reinforced canvas) and a partition in the middle (so as to host guests in the front of the tent and to have the back half as a comfortable living space). Once the PCs get a look inside the tent, read to them the following.

A bizarre place of opulence despite its isolation, the inside of this pavilion is divided by a curtain that runs from roof to floor. In the open front half, a massive, iron-banded wooden trunk rests along the north wall while a row of boxes lines the south wall. Four heavily cushioned leather chairs sit in the middle of the open space in pairs. A tall, wrought-iron candelabra stands in the center of the area, its twelve evenly spaced candles burning merrily and giving off a mixture of pleasant aromas.

This is where the PCs are brought when they show up in the camp. The thugs ask for the PCs' weapons before leading them in here to speak with the boss, but if a PC doesn't want to give up his weapon, the thugs don't press the matter. Zincher greets the PCs as detailed in the section "An Audience with Clegg," on page 35.

Treasure: Zincher keeps several of his most private personal and business possessions inside the large trunk—he generally takes this trunk with him wherever he goes, since he's loath to leave the contents untended by himself. The trunk itself is locked. Zincher carries the key, but the lock can be picked with a DC 30 Open Lock check.

Inside are several ledgers for all his businesses (legitimate and illicit), a ledger tracking his own personal (and considerable) wealth, and copies of deeds for the places he owns in Riddleport (the originals are all held in town). If Zincher survives a combat encounter with the PCs, the amount of information held within these documents can ruin him. Although they could be used by Magnimar or Korvosa to effect an arrest, if the contents were made public, the lords of Riddleport would act swiftly to put him down, since as these records plainly show, there's hardly anyone in the city who hasn't been double- or triple-crossed by Zincher at one point. Any of Riddleport's crimelords (or even the overlord himself) would gladly pay up to 8,000 gp for these documents (although they'd likely first offer a mere 1,000 gp). Unfortunately for greedy PCs, most of the deeds, IOUs, and other financial documents here are close to impossible to collect—with Zincher out of the picture, those who owe these debts find his death a perfect excuse to forget what was due.

Of greater interest to the PCs, the trunk also contains a rough map of Devil's Elbow. The map indicates all the sites where bits of noqual were found, but more importantly, a single "X" marks a spot on the southern shore along the cliffs not far from the campsite. This X reveals the location of the drow encampment.

In addition, beneath all the papers, Zincher keeps three large sacks holding 50 pp each and two small bags. One of the small bags contains eight beryls worth 40 gp apiece, and the other holds four rubies and a black pearl, all worth 100 gp each. Finally, the chest also contains several lumps of noqual ore—35 pounds of the stuff in all.

E7. Cages (EL 5)

Several crude wooden cages sit under the trees here. Each cage is empty.

Creatures: Zincher hoped to capture several akatas in these cages he had his men build, but so far hasn't managed to catch a single one. This area isn't uninhabited, though; he keeps three of his prized pets here: large, predatory, flightless birds known as axebeaks. The dangerous birds are trained and, while they won't attack Zincher or his men, they do rattle and squawk at anyone except Clegg who approaches too closely. The birds are tethered to the trees here by thick ropes tied to their left ankles, but the ropes give them 20 feet of mobility to attack anyone they don't recognize. If the birds come to harm, any chance of a peaceful meeting with Zincher is lost—he'll brutally murder anyone he knows hurt his pets.

Axebeaks (3)   CR 2

Tome of Horrors Revised 26

N Large animal

Init +3; **Senses** low-light vision, scent; Listen +5, Spot +5

DEFENSE

AC 14, touch 12, flat-footed 11

    (+3 Dex, +2 natural, −1 size)

hp 22 (3d8+9)

Fort +6, **Ref** +6, **Will** +1

OFFENSE

Spd 50 ft.

Melee 2 claws +5 (1d6+3) and

    bite +0 (1d6+1)

Space 10 ft.; **Reach** 10 ft.

TACTICS

During Combat The axebeaks focus their attacks on one

    character at a time—usually a character attacking Zincher.

Morale The axebeaks fight to the death to protect their

    master, even if he drops.

STATISTICS

Str 16, **Dex** 17, **Con** 16, **Int** 2, **Wis** 11, **Cha** 10

Base Atk +2; **Grp** +9

Feats Alertness, Weapon Focus (claw)

Skills Listen +5, Spot +5

An Audience with Clegg

Once the PCs secure an audience with Clegg Zincher, the man invites them to have a seat in one of the large chairs in his tent. If he's present, Erix stands at attention in a corner. At the very least, four of his thugs stand guard just outside of the tent flaps, which remain open as long as the meeting continues.

Zincher isn't particularly surprised to see the PCs—they've already made a name for themselves in Riddleport, after all. He greets the PCs as if they were old friends, commenting that they must be fearless—or perhaps desperate—adventurers indeed to brave the perils of Devil's Elbow simply to pay him a visit. Zincher rightfully fears the PCs and sees them as a threat—not as a physical threat to his well-being, but more as a threat to his hard-won empire—but does his best to hide his fear and remain calm. If they uncover his connection with the island's drow and report it in Riddleport, Zincher knows he's ruined. Thus, Zincher does his best to prevent the PCs from becoming too suspicious about his motives here.

What Zincher really wants from the PCs is for them to discover the drow and defeat them, thereby freeing him from his magically crafted obligation to them. Unfortunately for Zincher, that same magic prevents him from simply asking for help—worse, it amplifies his natural frustration, and if the PCs don't catch on to what he wants them to do, he may well fly into a rage. Zincher starts his conversation with the PCs by asking them why

CLEGG'S QUESTS

Clegg has three tasks in mind for the PCs. He can assign them in any order you wish, one at a time or all at once.

    Noqual Gathering: Clegg wants the PCs to gather noqual from the large crater site; he'll pay over full price (60 gp per pound) for any noqual the PCs recover for him.

    Catch a Live Akata: If the PCs can catch living akatas and keep them caged, Clegg promises them 500 gp for each. Of course, catching akatas and keeping them in simple wooden cages might prove troublesome.

    Defend the Camp: Two nights ago, a pair of void zombies attacked the camp. Last night, there were four. Clegg suspects these zombies were once members of the Cyphermages or even Slyeg's group, but the fact that each night brings more worries him. He promises each PC 50 gp per night spent guarding the camp. True to form, that night, a group of 1d6+2 void zombies attacks. Clegg, Erix, and any guards are on hand to help the PCs fight back the undead.

they're here, who sent them here, and what they expect and hope to find on Devil's Elbow. He's also curious to learn the fates of the other groups on the island, and is particularly keen to hear about any battles the PCs have had with akatas or void zombies.

Characters who speak with Zincher for at least a minute have a chance to notice he's charmed; make secret DC 25 Sense Motive checks for each PC to determine if they notice the magical effect's subtle influence on the man. If asked about the drow, Zincher is somewhat startled and shocked, but attempts to Bluff that he doesn't know anything about any drow on the island. He suffers a −4 circumstance penalty on his Bluff check the first time someone mentions drow to him. The effects of the charm prevent Zincher from admitting openly that he knows about the drow, or worse, that he's working for them. Pressing the man on the matter quickly makes him angry—if the PCs push too hard, he may even be provoked into attacking them, in which case his thugs come to his aid. If Erix has told the PCs the truth about his mission here, he aids them in defeating Zincher (attempting to catch him alive, if possible). Otherwise, the mercenary aids Zincher but pulls his punches against the PCs, hoping to knock them out rather than kill them.

Assuming the conversation doesn't frustrate Zincher into attacking, he eventually steers the conversation into the matter of the "unfortunate denizens of the island." By this, he of course means the drow, but he phrases it carefully so as to make the PCs think he's speaking of the void zombies or akatas. He mentions several possible tasks that the PCs could undertake for him, and he promises payments in gold for each successful mission (such funds payable upon his safe return to Riddleport,

of course). These missions are more than Zincher trying to recruit the PCs into helping him achieve his goals—he hopes the PCs stumble upon the drow during these missions and that the resulting conflict might absolve him of his enslavement. Of course, he can't directly tell the PCs to go to the sea cave to confront the drow, but he does hope that they find the cave on their own. And in the meantime, if they can catch some akatas for him or gather some noqual... all the better! He even offers to set the PCs up with their own tent, placing the tent between area **E5** and **E6**. Consult the sidebar on page 35 for the various missions Clegg has in mind.

If the PCs complete all the missions for Clegg but still haven't uncovered the location of the drow on the island, all is not lost. The charm effect on Zincher has a duration of only a few days; since Shindiira placed the initial *charm monster* on him, she's ordered him to meet her at area **G1** every night in secret so she can put additional *suggestions* on him to keep him from getting any ideas about betraying her. Clegg knows she's controlling him magically, but fears the drow so much that he goes along

with her demands. By inviting the PCs to stay in his camp and placing their tent near the trail that leads down to the caves, Clegg hopes that the PCs will notice him leaving one night and follow him down to the cave, at which point the confrontation he hopes will occur could finally set him free.

PART FIVE: ARCHITECTS OF RUIN

The drow of Devil's Elbow don't plan to remain on the island for much longer. Indeed, Shindiira would have left the place a few days ago, after they were done studying the meteorite and breaking it down into portable chunks for transport, but she's become fascinated by the akatas. Their skill at battle, combined with the fact that those they kill become zombies, makes them quite a desirable weapon—used against the elves of Celwynvian, akatas could become a key element in the battle for control of the ancient city. Shindiira is certain that if she returns to Celwynvian with tame akatas or living larvae in docile undead hosts, she will be greatly rewarded.

How long it takes Shindiira to accomplish her goals is up to you, but you shouldn't have her leave the island before the PCs make at least one attempt to confront her. If the PCs don't follow Zincher down to area **G1** on one of his midnight trips, having Erix open up to them and recruit their aid in trying to force out Zincher's secret is a great way to get them started down the path to the cave the drow dwell in. Even simple curiosity can suffice—noticing the hidden trail is possible with a DC 25 Spot check by anyone who spends at least 10 minutes wandering around the undergrowth surrounding Zincher's camp.

The cave system that the drow now inhabit was once the lair of a legendary local siren named Virashi. When the siren first came to Devil's Elbow more than 600 years ago, she spent several months exploring the island in search of a suitable home. Although she passed by this sea cave numerous times, at last she concluded nowhere else on the island would suit her, and she moved in. For hundreds of years, Virashi menaced ships that came into the lagoon or approached the island too closely, luring in unfortunate and foolish sailors with her dire magic until she was at last slain by an angry mob. Her ghost dwells in the cave now, but the drow have effectively isolated her to one cave and have free run of the rest of the complex.

G1. The Cliffside Path

Once the hidden path reaches the cliffside here, it becomes a bit more obvious; following it is a simple matter. It can be spotted from sea only with a DC 30 Spot check, though. Only 5 feet wide, the narrow ledge winds down the cliffside until finally ending at a spur of rock some 20 feet above the sea below. If the PCs are following Zincher, he pretends not to notice them unless they're too obvious about following him or openly try to contact him, at which point he's forced to lie that he came down here to do some fishing. The lie is a tough sell—Zincher suffers a –6 penalty to his Bluff check since he's not carrying a fishing pole. If the PCs remain unseen, Zincher makes it all the way to area **G2**, knocks on the wall, then steps into a hole in the cliffside after a secret door opens. He goes on to meet Shindiira in area **G3**, remaining in there for only a few minutes before she finishes with him and sends him back up to the camp.

G2. Hidden Entrance (CR 4)

Virashi had the only land entrance into her lair obscured by a secret door built by an enraptured dwarf sailor she caught many centuries ago. The secret door can be found with a DC 20 Search check, but it is protected by a trap placed there by Shindiira.

The narrow fissure opening into area **G7** from the cliffside is difficult to notice, requiring a DC 25 Spot check (remember to account for distance penalties).

Trap: A *glyph of warding* guards the secret door—it activates if any non-evil creature opens the door.

GLYPH OF WARDING   CR 4
Type spell; **Search** DC 28; **Disable Device** DC 28
EFFECTS
Trigger spell; **Reset** none
Effect spell effect (*glyph of warding* [blast], 5th-level cleric, 2d8 sonic, DC 16 Reflex half damage); multiple targets (all targets within 5 ft.)

G3. Entry Chamber (EL 6)

Water drips down along the walls of this damp cavern. The cave itself is cluttered with bits of rubble and debris, much of which seems to be from a strange, blackened form of rock quite different in appearance from the rock that makes up the walls of the cavern. The ceiling slopes up to the north, from a height of about ten feet near the southern exit to a height of twenty-five feet to the north.

The strange rubble in this room is all that remains of the stony portion of the meteorite the drow called down from the skies. They removed the largest fragments from the crater and returned with them here, then broke away all of the portions of the meteorite that contained noqual ore and stored the ore in area **G9g**. Anyone who's seen smaller fragments of the meteorite ore can notice the similarity of the burnt stone fragments here automatically.

Creatures: Two drow guards are stationed here, standing sentinel against the southeast and northeast walls. Unless Xakihn has raised the alarm already (see area **G7**), the drow notice the PCs' approach if they make successful Listen checks, or automatically if the secret door is opened during the day and thus floods the room with light.

DROW GUARDS (2)   CR 4
Male drow fighter 3
CE Medium humanoid (elf)
Init +3; **Senses** darkvision 120 ft.; Listen +6, Spot +6
DEFENSE
AC 18, touch 13, flat-footed 15
    (+4 armor, +3 Dex, +1 shield)
hp 24 (3d10+3)
Fort +4, **Ref** +4, **Will** +2 (+2 against spells and spell-like abilities); +2 against enchantment
Immune sleep; **SR** 14
Weaknesses light blindness

Sea Caves

1 square = 5 feet

OFFENSE

Spd 30 ft.

Melee mwk rapier +8 (1d6+1)

Ranged mwk hand crossbow +7 (1d4/19–20)

Spell-Like Abilities (CL 3rd)

1/day—*dancing lights, darkness, faerie fire*

TACTICS

During Combat The drow guards attack as soon as they notice anyone entering the cave. One moves up to block the entrance to the cave and fights with his rapier, while the other hangs back and uses his crossbow against spellcasters in an attempt to disrupt spellcasting.

Morale In the hope of gaining recognition for their abilities, these drow continue to fight even in the face of overwhelming odds. Once reduced to 10 hp, though, a drow realizes he's outmatched and starts a fighting retreat toward area **G9**, calling for aid from other allies positioned in chambers along the way.

STATISTICS

Str 13, **Dex** 17, **Con** 12, **Int** 10, **Wis** 12, **Cha** 12

Base Atk +3; **Grp** +4

Feats Dodge, Mobility, Weapon Finesse, Weapon Focus (rapier)

Skills Climb +7, Listen +6, Search +2, Spot +6

Languages Common, Elven, Undercommon

Combat Gear *potion of cure light wounds*; **Other Gear** masterwork chain shirt, masterwork small steel shield, masterwork rapier, masterwork hand crossbow with 10 bolts

G4. Collapsed Tunnel

The tunnel here once led directly to the now-destroyed chamber for the glyphs used to call down the fallen star, but the impact caused it to collapse at several points along its route.

G5. Virashi's Prison (EL 7)

When the drow first came to Devil's Elbow and discovered this cave, everything seemed perfect about the site as a base of operations save for one small detail—this cave was haunted by the ghost of the siren Virashi. Shindiira was assigned to this island primarily for her skill at crafting magic items—the creation of a barricade that would isolate the siren and her song was her first project. This barricade appears as a wall of wood covered with spidery runes in Undercommon warning of great undead peril beyond the barrier. Itself a magic item, the barricade fills the chamber beyond with magical silence to suppress the siren's dangerous song—there was no real need to use more potent magic to hedge the ghost in, since she cannot leave the site of her death. The barricade can be pried out of place with a DC 25 Strength check, or battered through with enough damage (hp 30; hardness 5). Either effect destroys the barrier's silence aura and exposes the complex and anyone inside it to the siren's song.

This large chamber rises to a height of roughly thirty feet near the center, where a very small hole acts as a natural skylight. Relatively quiet, with the constant crash of the ocean muffled by solid stone, this cave seems an ideal lair. Moisture-slicked mildewing tapestries and animal pelts cover nearly every inch of the walls, indicating that at one time this chamber did serve as home to some kind of creature.

Creature: Long before the drow came to Devil's Elbow, Virashi the siren called this cave complex home. This chamber served as her main living area, and the rotting tapestries and pelts consist of her ancient attempts to use various salvaged materials and flotsam washed ashore from shipwrecks to bring an air of opulence to the cave. Since she was slain many years ago, Virashi's ghost has been bound to this cavern, the site of her death, as a ghost.

Virashi's continued existence on the Material Plane is a tale of tragedy and despair, for she pines for the one true love she lost so many years ago. Until she discovers his fate, she refuses to allow her soul to move on into the afterlife. When the drow arrived and set up camp, Virashi hoped they might have the information for which she longs. Upon approaching them, they attacked and "slew" her, and when she rejuvenated several days later, rage filled her mind and she lashed out at the drow in her cave, forcing the intruder elves to isolate her with a magical barricade. Unable to move beyond the boundaries of this chamber, Virashi has spent the past several weeks suffering the drow's proximity while she spends all hours of the day and night in torment.

Fortunately for the PCs, Virashi's wrath has simmered to a cool burn, and if they remove the barrier and enter her lair, the ghostly siren is merely indifferent to their presence. She recognizes them as non-drow and does not hold against them the earlier actions of the dark elves,

and hopes that these new intruders might have news of her lost love.

Soon after the PCs remove the silence barrier, Virashi manifests as a ghostly bird-like creature with the head of a beautiful woman. She cries out in a woeful voice, "Where is my Yaris? What has happened to him?"

Any character who makes a DC 20 Knowledge (history) check, or who heard the story of how Yaris threw himself from the eastern tower (perhaps from Captain Creesy or their own early investigations into Devil's Elbow), can answer Virashi's lament. Allow the character a Diplomacy check to adjust the ghost's initial attitude of unfriendly— if the character wishes to attempt to make up a story, he'll first need to successfully bluff the ghost before he can make this Diplomacy check.

If the PCs can make Virashi indifferent, she'll answer questions they have about the drow. She's unable to leave this cave, and as a result, her insights into what the drow are doing here are limited, but she can certainly describe the standard drow guard, Xakihn, Shindiira, and the shadow demon Chmetugo. She won't aid the PCs unless they make her at least friendly, though, in which case she agrees to use her siren song in any way the PCs wish to attack the drow. Note that the PCs must use *silence* or other methods to protect themselves from her song if they take this option against the drow.

If the characters fail to soothe Virashi's growing anger with an explanation of what became of Yaris (be it a clever lie or the truth), she attacks after 2d4 rounds.

Virashi

VIRASHI   CR 7

Female siren ghost (MM 117, *Pathfinder* #14 84)

CN Medium undead (incorporeal)

Init +4; **Senses** darkvision 60 ft., low-light vision; Listen +23, Spot +23

DEFENSE

AC 21, touch 21, flat-footed 17
  (+7 deflection, +4 Dex)

hp 52 (8d12)

Fort +6, **Ref** +12, **Will** +6

Defensive Abilities incorporeal traits, +4 turn resistance;
  Immune mind-affecting effects

OFFENSE

Spd fly 60 ft. (perfect)

Melee corrupting touch +12 (1d6)

A HELPFUL GHOST

Not every encounter in a dungeon needs to be a fight. The encounter with Virashi is a great example; not only is she a powerful foe, but simply fighting her isn't going to accomplish anything; she has no treasure to loot, and if destroyed she'll simply reform in a few days. The real purpose here is to give the PCs a chance to learn a little bit about the recent history of the caves and to give them a potent ally and weapon that they can use against the drow—Virashi's songs can wreak havoc on drow teamwork, granting the PCs what may be a key advantage over them. Alternatively, if the PCs have laid Yaris' spirit to rest, Virashi is perhaps even more helpful in granting them her blessing before moving on.

—James Jacobs

Special Attacks bardic music, frightful moan (DC 21), manifestation, siren song

Spell-Like Abilities (CL 7th)

3/day—*cause fear* (DC 18), *charm person* (DC 18), *deep slumber* (DC 20), *shout* (DC 21)

TACTICS

During Combat Virashi relies on charmed or obsessed creatures to protect her in battle, since beyond her *shout* spell-like ability she doesn't have a very strong offensive. Against a single foe, she attempts to captivate them, then shreds them to ribbons with her corrupting touch.

Morale Virashi fights until destroyed.

STATISTICS

Str 10, **Dex** 19, **Con** —, **Int** 14, **Wis** 19, **Cha** 25

Base Atk +8; **Grp** +8

Feats Dodge, Flyby Attack, Lightning Reflexes

Skills Hide +17, Knowledge (history) +8, Listen +23, Perform (sing) +18, Search +10, Spot +23

Languages Auran, Common

SQ rejuvenation

SPECIAL ABILITIES

Rejuvenation (Su) As long as her lover Yaris remains bound to this world as a wraith, Virashi rejuvenates 2d4 days after she is destroyed if she makes a DC 16 level check.

Development: Although Virashi's ghost is bound to this world as long as the restless spirit of her lover Yaris remains a wraith, if the PCs defeat the wraith at area **F**, Virashi lingers here for a few days. When the PCs arrive, she can sense echoes of Yaris's troubled soul in them. She felt his release from undeath as he was defeated by the PCs, and lingered here only so she could grant her blessing to the PCs, should they come by.

If the PCs enter this room after having defeated Yaris, they find a much different ghost than the one detailed above. In this case, Virashi is quiet, calm, and serene when the PCs meet her. She smiles radiantly as she sees them, greeting them as "the saviors of my beloved's soul." She goes on to thank them for allowing Yaris's angry wraith to finally escape this world and move on, and says that now he is no longer bound to this world by anger, she is no longer bound here by grief. She thanks the PCs again, and then with a sudden flare of white light, she is gone. Her departure invests a magical blessing in the PCs. For the remainder of this adventure, they gain a +4 morale bonus on all saving throws against mind-affecting effects and a +2 morale bonus on all attack rolls and skill checks.

Ad-Hoc Experience Award: If the PCs befriend Virashi and gain her aid in defeating the drow, award them experience as if they had defeated her in combat.

G6. Haunt of Shadows (EL 7)

Creature: This intersection is the current lair of Shindiira's most powerful ally, Chmetugo the shadow demon. Once a powerful demon in the service of Nocticula, the Demon Lady of Darkness and Lust, Chmetugo had the audacity to spurn a powerful succubus, who in retaliation used her considerable pull in Nocticula's court to have Chmetugo exiled to the Material Plane. The shadow demon's exile has lasted for only 3 years so far, but already he has learned to loathe the plane and its accursed brightness with a hatred even he didn't think was possible. Shindiira encountered him in Celwynvian and secured his allegiance with promises to figure out a way to return him to the Abyss eventually—although Chmetugo knows better than to take her at her word, she is a priestess of Nocticula, and if he can satisfy her needs as a guardian and minion, certainly that can only help reverse his unfair exile. The demon spends much of his time constructing elaborate scenarios in his mind on the torments and vengeances he will inflict on the succubus who had him exiled. This chamber is his favorite place to lurk, since its central location allows the demon to respond to alarms anywhere in the complex with relative speed.

CHMETUGO   CR 7

Shadow demon (*Tome of Horrors Revised* 129)

CE Medium outsider (chaotic, evil, demon, extraplanar, incorporeal)

Init +7; **Senses** darkvision 60 ft.; Listen +14, Spot +14

DEFENSE

AC 15, touch 15, flat-footed 13

(+3 deflection, +2 Dex)

hp 52 (7d8+21)

Fort +8, **Ref** +8, **Will** +7

Defensive Abilities incorporeal traits; **Immune** electricity, poison; **Resist** acid 10, cold 10, fire 10

Weaknesses sunlight powerlessness

OFFENSE

Spd fly 40 ft. (perfect)

Melee 2 incorporeal claws +10 (1d6) and incorporeal bite +5 (1d8)

Special Attacks pounce, rake 1d6

Spell-Like Abilities (CL 10th)

1/day—*deeper darkness*, *fear* (DC 17)

1/week—*magic jar* (DC 18; already used)

TACTICS

During Combat Chmetugo begins combat with a charge attack, pouncing with a bloodcurdling shriek on the first intruder he spies. He saves his *fear* ability to use if he becomes overwhelmed by foes, and *deeper darkness* to cover his escape if he needs to flee. He's already used *magic jar* to possess one of the dwarven prospectors, but his "joy ride" ended with the dwarf's death by an akata; if the PCs take more than 6 days to confront the shadow demon, he regains the use of this ability and uses it to seize control of one of the party healers to attack the group.

Morale Once reduced to half his hit points, Chmetugo uses *deeper darkness* to try to flee to Shindiira's side. He sees her as his ticket home, and won't flee as long as she lives—as soon as she dies, though, the demon abandons Devil's Elbow and heads south to look for a new patron.

STATISTICS

Str —, **Dex** 17, **Con** 17, **Int** 14, **Wis** 14, **Cha** 16

Base Atk +7; **Grp** —

Feats Alertness, Blind-Fight, Improved Initiative

Skills Bluff +13, Hide +13, Intimidate +15, Knowledge (dungeoneering) +12, Knowledge (religion) +12, Knowledge (the planes) +12, Listen +14, Search +12, Sense Motive +12, Spot +14, Survival +12

Languages Abyssal, Common, Elven, Undercommon; telepathy 100 ft.

SQ quick sprint, shadow blend

SPECIAL ABILITIES

Pounce (Ex) If a shadow demon charges, it can make a full attack, including two rake attacks.

Quick Sprint (Ex) Once per minute, a shadow demon may rapidly beat its incorporeal wings. This allows it to move at six times its normal speed (240 feet) for one round.

Rake (Ex) Attack bonus +10 melee touch, damage 1d6.

Shadow Blend (Su) During any conditions other than full daylight, a shadow demon can disappear into the shadows, giving it total concealment. Artificial illumination, even a *light* or *continual flame* spell, does not negate this ability; a *daylight* spell, however, will.

Sunlight Powerlessness (Su) Shadow demons are utterly powerless in natural sunlight (not merely a *daylight* spell) and flee from it. A shadow demon caught in sunlight cannot attack and can take only a single move or attack action.

G7. Observation Post (EL 5)

The sound of waves crashing against the cliffs echoes in this chamber through a narrow fissure in the eastern wall. A low table sits against the west wall, on which the remains of an unusual creature are splayed. The doglike beast's body is partially dissected and surrounded by a variety of tools and half-filled bottles.

Thanks to its position and the narrow shelf it opens onto, this chamber serves as a perfect place to watch the land approach to the caves, providing an unobstructed view all the way up the cliffside without appearing obvious from outside.

The body on the makeshift table is, of course, a dead akata that Xakihn has been examining. He's fascinated by the monsters and hoped that if he could learn about their inner workings, he'd be able to command them as surely as he commands terrestrial animals to do his bidding. Unfortunately, his examination only confirmed his fears that the creatures are just too alien for his magic to have much sway over. The body itself is partially melted in places, and the entire thing is covered with blisters and lesions—results of exposure to salt water. Xakihn's current goal is to gather several live akatas and then transport them back to Celwynvian so he can unleash the creatures on the mainland. He's captured a few so far, but none of them survived his examinations. Lately, he's decided a safer and more efficient route is to simply let Zincher pursue his similar goals, and then swoop in to take any captured akatas from him when the time comes to leave Devil's Elbow.

Creature: Xakihn is an unusual drow, even by drow standards. He has dwelt for many years on the surface, living in the wild deep in the Mierani Forest where he became a student of the cruelty of nature. The wasp that paralyzes the tarantula to be a living banquet for her young, the cat who torments the mouse before eating it, and the savage fury of a man-eating bear are all fascinating subjects to the drow, who has come to think of the dark and cruel woodlands as his true home. The sun still gives him headaches, but deep under tangled forest canopies it's not so bad. Always something of an outsider, he isn't officially affiliated with the drow of Celwynvian, but they secured his aid early on when it became apparent that his knowledge of the region was invaluable. He volunteered for the mission to Devil's Elbow simply because the prospect of being so close to a fallen star was something he couldn't miss. He and his animal companion, a foul-tempered albino giant gecko named Theyardlyn, relocate to area **G9d** as soon as they see the PCs.

Xakihn

Xakihn   CR 5

Male drow druid 4

NE Medium humanoid (elf)

Init +2; **Senses** darkvision 120 ft.; Listen +12, Spot +12

DEFENSE

AC 16, touch 12, flat-footed 14

(+2 armor, +2 Dex, +2 natural)

hp 25 (4d8+4)

Fort +5, **Ref** +5, **Will** +7 (+9 against spells); +2 against enchantments

Defensive Abilities resist nature's lure; **Immune** sleep; **SR** 15

Weaknesses light blindness

OFFENSE

Spd 30 ft.

Melee +1 *spear* +5 (1d8+2/×3)

Ranged mwk dagger +6 (1d4+1/19–20)

Spell-Like Abilities (CL 4th)

1/day—*dancing lights, darkness, faerie fire*

Spells Prepared (CL 4th, +5 ranged touch)

2nd—*barkskin, flame blade, summon swarm*

1st—*charm animal* (DC 14), *cure light wounds, jump, obscuring mist*

0—*cure minor wounds* (3), *guidance, mending*

TACTICS

Before Combat Xakihn casts *barkskin* on himself as soon as he knows the PCs are approaching.

During Combat Xakihn uses his *wand of produce flame* at range, switching to his spear if enemies get within 10 feet and then casting *flame blade* (holding his spear in his off hand) if foes get inside his spear's reach. He uses spells like *summon swarm* or *obscuring mist* to distract enemies that use ranged attacks against him.

Morale Xakihn and Theyardlyn fight until Xakihn is reduced to half his hit points, at which time they both flee to Shindiira's side.

STATISTICS

Str 12, **Dex** 15, **Con** 12, **Int** 12, **Wis** 16, **Cha** 10

Base Atk +3; **Grp** +4

Feats Combat Casting, Lightning Reflexes

Skills Concentration +8, Handle Animal +7, Knowledge (nature) +10, Listen +12, Search +3, Spot +12

Languages Common, Druidic, Elven, Sylvan, Undercommon

SQ animal companion, nature sense, trackless step, wild empathy +6, woodland stride

Combat Gear *wand of produce flame* (24 charges); **Other Gear** masterwork leather armor, *+1 spear*, masterwork dagger, two silver bracelets worth 50 gp each, silver ring worth 100 gp

---

THEYARDLYN   CR —

Male giant gecko animal companion (*Pathfinder* #1 89)

N Medium animal

Init +7; **Senses** darkvision 120 ft., low-light vision, scent; Listen +2, Spot +2

DEFENSE

AC 17, touch 13, flat-footed 14

(+3 Dex, +4 natural)

hp 22 (4d8+4)

Fort +5, **Ref** +7, **Will** +3

Defensive Abilities evasion

OFFENSE

Spd 40 ft., climb 40 ft.

Melee bite +6 (2d4+3)

TACTICS

During Combat Theyardlyn remains within 5 feet of his master if he can, biting anyone who comes within reach.

Morale As long as Xakihn lives, Theyardlyn fights to the death. If his master dies, Theyardlyn flees if brought below 10 hit points.

STATISTICS

Str 14, **Dex** 17, **Con** 12, **Int** 2, **Wis** 14, **Cha** 6

Base Atk +3; **Grp** +5

Feats Improved Initiative, Weapon Focus (bite)

Skills Balance +11, Climb +25

SQ expert climber, link, share spells

SPECIAL ABILITIES

Expert Climber (Ex) Theyardlyn can climb any surface as if he were under the effects of a *spider climb* spell. He has a +8 racial bonus and further +8 untyped bonus on Climb checks.

G8. Barracks (EL 6)

Six net hammocks supported by ornate metal frames made level by stacks of stone stand around the edges of this cavern. To the west, a leather curtain hangs over an exit, through which the sound of churning waves rumbles. A ledge to the south rises twenty feet to a second passageway there, while the ceiling itself arches to a vaulted height of forty feet.

This chamber serves as a barracks for the six drow guards who remain on Devil's Elbow. At any one time, two drow are at rest here. If the alarm is raised, they relocate to area **G9a** to aid the drow stationed there; otherwise, they are asleep in hammocks.

DROW GUARDS (2)   CR 4

hp 24 each (see page 37)

G9. Sea Cave (EL 9)

Several thick, rocky natural pillars rise up in this high sea cave. The water filling the lower portion of the enormous cavern sloshes and surges with the tide, and a five-foot-wide rocky beach lines the northeastern face of the pool. The cave ceiling soars to a height of eighty feet. To the south, several wooden platforms attached to the rock pillars are further supported by wooden pilings—the structure looks somewhat treacherous. The sound of rushing, falling water comes from the northern end of the chamber, where a thin cascade of water plummets from a narrow crack in the ceiling into the pool below.

The entrance to this sea cave opens directly to the ocean. At high tide, the entrance is completely submerged and the sea cave's rocky beaches are reduced to narrow slivers. With the entrance blocked, the chamber falls into darkness the drow find comforting. At low tide, a gap of nearly 2 feet exists between the top of the entrance and the ocean's surface. The dotted lines on the map show the extent of the affected area of the southern entrance.

The wooden platforms built up throughout the chamber are made from the wreckage of several ships that have wrecked on the reefs surrounding the island—the platforms are all that remains of a once larger structure formerly inhabited by a tribe of goblins that served Virashi nearly 50 years ago. The goblins have long gone, but the remnants of their lair remain, and despite the age of the materials and rot around the edges, the platforms and rope-and-plank bridges are

THE SEA CAVE

The following key areas are found in the Sea Cave.

G9a. Low Platform: A ladder leads up 10 feet to this first platform. If the drow from area **G8** have moved into this cavern, they take up position here.

G9b. Central Platform: This platform is 15 feet above the water; the bridge leading here from area **G9a** slants upward to this location.

G9c. Western Platform: A hand-cranked rope-and-pulley system allows someone on this platform to raise or lower gear from the supply cache at **G9e** below. This platform is 15 feet above the water.

G9d. Main Platform: This large platform is 20 feet above the water below. Two drow guards are stationed here. A small box near the wall contains some treasure (see area **G9** for details).

G9e. Supply Cache: Supplies and gear are stored on this high beach; see area **G9** for details.

G9f. Waterfall: The sound of this waterfall is quite loud within 15 feet; Listen checks made in this area suffer a −4 penalty.

G9g. Shindiira's Ledge: This ledge is 50 feet above the water below. Shindiira has taken up residence here; she sleeps in a hammock strung from a pair of iron hooks she embedded in the walls via *stone shape* spells. A darkwood trunk sits on the ledge as well—Shindiira's personal treasure (see area **G9**).

sturdy and dependable now that the drow have repaired and reinforced them in places.

The water in the cave drops quickly beyond the rocky beaches. In the squares adjacent to the beaches, the water is 2 feet deep, but beyond that, it quickly plummets into a 25-foot-deep pool.

Listen checks made in this cave suffer a −2 penalty due to the sloshing of the water from the waves and waterfall.

Creatures: This chamber is the lair of the current leader of the drow who remain here—Shindiira Misraria. In addition to her, two other drow are stationed in this room as guards, and an orca whale that's been charmed by Xakihn swims lazily in the waters of the pool, waiting for another offering of meat or the chance to serve his dark masters. Depending on how the fights in the eastern portion of the cavern went, there may be additional creatures awaiting the PCs here as well.

Shindiira busies herself with sorting her belongings and packing them into a darkwood trunk as she readies for the return journey to Celwynvian, once Clegg Zincher manages to catch a healthy number of akatas and accumulates a bit more noqual. She's basically finished her studies and observations of the fallen star and its effects; she doesn't completely understand how the weapon works, but made sure to take detailed notes in the days after the event so that her superiors in Celwynvian will be as best supplied with intelligence as possible.

Not immune to the natural beauty of the place, Shindiira chose this chamber as her home. She is an unnervingly quiet drow with a piercing gaze. Dark, wavy tattoos grace her cheeks, shoulders, and hips. She conducts herself with stoic resolve and does not shout challenges or otherwise call out to the PCs while fighting them. She remains resolutely silent.

Shindiira belongs to House Misraria, a lesser drow noble house in the city of Zirnakaynin that has long had allegiances to the more powerful House Azrinae. House Misraria venerates Nocticula, the Demon Lady of Darkness and Lust, and her faithful often become hired killers; many (though not all) take levels in assassin, but all choose a weapon that they feel best embodies the art of the kill for their own personality. Shindiira's choice was the flail, a weapon that requires both grace and strength to wield and can wrench a foe's weapon from his hand, pull him from his feet, or bash in his skull depending on the wielder's whim. Shindiira is quite proud of her skill with the flail, and prefers to disarm foes, trip them, and then strike for the kill.

When Allevrah Azrinae arrived in Zirnakaynin several years ago and seized control of House Azrinae, a violent schism struck House Misraria. Some of the disciples of Nocticula wanted to side with Allevrah, while others saw this as a chance to strike at the stronger house while it was distracted and perhaps seize its role of power in the city government. In the end, House Misraria nearly collapsed due to internal strife, and Shindiira decided to abandon her family and offered her services to the Azrinaes.

She was taken in by a drow named Depora, and the two of them quickly found that their appetites for inflicting pain on others were even more enjoyable when they shared the inflicting. They became almost as sisters, so when Depora was ordered to travel to the surface to aid the Azrinaes in Celwynvian, Shindiira saw it not only as a grand adventure, but also as a chance to bring Nocticula's wrath to all manner of new and unsuspecting victims.

Yet not long after they arrived in Celwynvian, their relationship began to sour, as all sisterhoods do in drow society. Both women became infatuated with the leader of the Azrinae efforts in Celwynvian (a wizard named Nolveniss), and competed for his time and companionship. Nolveniss enjoyed the companionship at first, but his nervous fear at being the focus of such attention resulted in his selection of the two drow as the ones to lead the expedition to Devil's Elbow and Riddleport in order to set up the targeting glyphs for the weapon and secure a portion of the Cyphergate arch for the final stage of his own experiments with a mysterious event called the Armageddon Echo. Separated from Nolveniss and forced to work together, the two drow increasingly bickered and fought. Eventually, Depora relocated to Riddleport to handle the secondary mission on her own, forcing Shindiira to remain on the island and possibly face unanticipated consequences should the fallen star prove bigger than anticipated.

Now that the weapon has been fired, Shindiira hopes that her return to Celwynvian with noqual and several akatas will afford her the status and respect to claim Nolveniss as her consort, and thus assume control over the operations in Celwynvian. Her only fear is that Depora will get there first with her Cyphergate fragment and beat her to the punch.

SHINDIIRA MISRARIA CR 7

Female drow cleric 5/fighter 1
CE Medium humanoid (elf)
Init +1; Senses darkvision 120 ft.;
 Listen +5, Spot +5

DEFENSE

AC 23, touch 13, flat-footed 22
 (+7 armor, +2 deflection, +1
 Dex, +3 shield)
hp 49 (6 HD; 5d8+1d10+18)
Fort +9, Ref +2, Will +7 (+9
 against spells and spell-
 like abilities); +2 against
 enchantment
Immune sleep; SR 17
Weaknesses light blindness

OFFENSE

Spd 30 ft.
Melee +1 flail +8 (1d8+4)
Ranged mwk hand crossbow +6 (1d4+1/19–20 plus
 poison)
Special Attacks rebuke undead 3/day (+2, 2d6+5)
Spell-Like Abilities (CL 5th)
 1/day—dancing lights, darkness, detect magic, faerie fire,
 feather fall, levitate
Spells Prepared (CL 5th; CL 6th with chaos spells)
 3rd—dispel magic, suggestion^D (DC 16), water walk
 2nd—bull's strength, bear's endurance, shatter^D (DC 15), silence
 1st—charm person^D (DC 14), command (DC 14), divine favor,
  protection from law^C, shield of faith
 0—create water, cure minor wounds (3), purify food and drink
 C chaos spell; D domain spell; Domains Chaos, Charm

TACTICS

Before Combat Once the PCs enter this area, the drow guards signal to Shindiira, who, in area G9g behind the northernmost pillar of stone, is out of sight of the entrances to the cave. She casts water walk, bull's strength, bear's endurance, protection from law, and shield of faith on herself before entering combat.

During Combat If the PCs come into view of her ledge

DEPORA'S RETURN

If Depora Azrinae survived the previous adventure and managed to escape back to Devil's Elbow, the PCs will encounter her here as well. She'll have claimed area G9d as her own, forcing the two drow guards there to relocate to area G9c, and her relationship with Shindiira has only grown more strained. Depending on how her fight with the PCs turned out, Depora is either aching for a rematch against them or exulting in her daring escape; in either case, Shindiira sees the PCs as an opportunity to finally get rid of her now-hated ally. When the PCs attack, Shindiira sides with the PCs and aids them in the fight against Depora, who shrieks in rage at the betrayal and then ignores the PCs to focus her attacks on Shindiira. The PCs shouldn't grow too accustomed to their apparent alliance, though, as both drow see them as problems. No matter who wins in the fight between Depora and Shindiira, the winner immediately turns her attention to the PCs and attempts to finish them off.

before she finishes casting her preparatory spells, she uses ranged magic against them, otherwise she feather falls down to the water to fight from its surface. She uses suggestion to force a PC to take a swim in the water (exposing them to the orca's attacks), and isn't afraid to cast shatter on a key support of a walkway while a PC stands on it. If she gets the chance, she casts divine favor just before entering combat. Her favorite melee tactic is to disarm foes before attacking them.

Morale Shindiira has fought her entire life in the service of Nocticula and does not fear death. She fights until slain.

Base Statistics AC 21, touch 11, flat-footed 22; hp 37;
 Fort +7; Melee +1 flail +6 (1d8+2); Str 13, Con 12; Skills
 Concentration +9

STATISTICS

Str 17, Dex 12, Con 16, Int 14, Wis 16, Cha 10
Base Atk +4; Grp +5
Feats Combat Expertise, Craft Wondrous Item, Dark Adept,
 Improved Disarm
Skills Concentration +11, Intimidate +4, Knowledge (arcana)
 +10, Knowledge (religion) +10, Spellcraft +12
Languages Common, Elven, Undercommon
SQ charm domain
Combat Gear wand of cure light wounds (32 charges), scroll of
 charm monster (2), drow sleep poison (10 doses); Other Gear
 +1 banded mail, +1 heavy steel shield, +1 flail, masterwork

DARK ADEPT

You gain additional spell-like abilities from your heritage.

Prerequisites: Drow, character level 3rd

Benefit: You gain three new spell-like abilities, each usable once per day. These spell-like abilities are *detect magic*, *feather fall*, and *levitate*. Your caster level for these spell-like abilities equals your total character level.

---

hand crossbow with 10 +1 bolts, *cloak of resistance +1*, silver circlet worth 350 gp

SPECIAL ABILITIES

Charm Domain (Su) Shindiira can boost her Charisma by 4 points once per day as a free action. This boost lasts for 1 minute.

DROW GUARDS (2)   CR 4
hp 24 each (see page 37)

ORCA   CR 5
hp 88 (MM 283)

Treasure: The goods stored at area **G9c** are primarily tools and supplies the drow used to move the meteorite from the crater to this area, to repair the platforms here, and other sundry supplies needed to create the now destroyed targeting chamber to the north. The supplies include two block and tackles, 10 square yards of canvas, 50 feet of chain, five crowbars, three fishing nets, six grappling hooks, four hammers, six hooded lanterns, a set of masterwork shipwright's tools, a set of masterwork carpenter's tools, a set of masterwork tailor's tools, a merchant's scale, seven miner's picks, 14 pitons, two 10-foot poles, a portable ram, 200 feet of silk rope, 17 empty sacks, and two sledges. Mixed in with all this mundane gear is a crate containing four bottles of 4663-vintage wine from the Terverius Wineries of southern Cheliax. Each bottle is worth 300 gp.

A small, unlocked box on the main platform (area **G9d**) contains two *potions of lesser restoration*, three *potions of remove paralysis*, five *potions of cure moderate wounds*, and a *potion of neutralize poison*. All are labeled in Undercommon.

Shindiira's trunk (area **G9g**) contains more than just the 53 pounds of noqual harvested from the meteorite. This ore creates a rough layer along the bottom of the chest; atop it Shindiira has laid several changes of clothes (including two sets of noble outfits sized for an elven woman and worth 60 gp each) and a set of ostentatious costume jewelry worth 5 gp. Also in the chest is a silver scrolltube worth 150 gp that contains several maps—Devil's Elbow (before and after the meteorite strike), Riddleport, Celwynvian, western Varisia, and all of Varisia. The map of Celwynvian could be of particular

import to the Shin'Rakorath, as it includes information on several key drow encampments and patrol routes (see *Pathfinder* #15).

Perhaps the greatest treasure in the chests, though, are the three books wrapped in silk and leather and set along the left side of the chest. The first of these books is *Tsalkaean's Bestiary*, a book written in Undercommon that grants a +2 circumstance bonus on Knowledge (dungeoneering) checks to identify aberrations and oozes and is worth 200 gp. The second is a well-read book called *Thoughts on Varisian Customs*, written in Common and worth 10 gp.

The final book is a slender journal, similar in style to the one that Depora kept. Whereas Depora's journal made no mention of Shindiira, this journal mentions Depora many times. A character who reads the journal learns first of Shindiira's excitement at being accepted into House Azrinae, and then eventually her frustration and finally hatred for Depora. Nolveniss is mentioned by name several times as well; Shindiira is quite explicit in the ways in which she plans to use him as her consort once she returns to him in Celwynvian with a large amount of noqual and akatas to show him her power. The last dozen entries display a dramatic shift in tone, becoming an almost scientific list of observations of the strange meteorological effects that preceded the falling star, the impact itself, and developments afterward. The PCs can use these entries to piece together much of what's been going on over the past few days on the island. More importantly, the journal mentions several times an ominously titled event or object called an "Armageddon Echo"—information that the Shin'Rakorath will find quite intriguing at the start of the next adventure.

CONCLUDING THE ADVENTURE

The PCs' primary goal during "Children of the Void" is to confront the drow in the sea caves and recover Shindiira's papers and journals—the contents of these documents are incredibly valuable to the elves of Crying Leaf and the Mierani Forest, and when Kwava and his superiors find out they exist, they'll swiftly recruit the PCs to thier cause, as detailed at the start of the next adventure. Beyond this, the contents should also entice and intrigue the PCs—knowledge that the drow have a strong presence in the ruined elven city of Celwynvian should come as something of a shock. While the borders to this ancient city have been closed by the elves of the region for some time, they had, until now, done an excellent job at hiding the exact reasons for the closure. That the drow have such a strong presence in the ruins raises many questions.

Yet there are many other sub-quests for the PCs to complete on Devil's Elbow, and these quests can continue to provide adventure even after they confront the drow. For sake of ease, the major quests (and the rewards the PCs can reap for their completion) are listed here.

Defeat the Akata Menace: Surrounded by salt water and due to the island's normally low population, Devil's Elbow works quite effectively as a prison for the akatas—Golarion is fortunate that fate cast them down here rather than onto the mainland. It's up to you to decide how many void zombies and akatas are on the island, but if the PCs make the effort to exterminate them all and succeed, award them an ad hoc experience award as if they had defeated a CR 5 creature in combat.

Deliver Noqual to Riddleport: All of Riddleport's crimelords want to be the sole source of noqual once it becomes apparent that the precious skymetal is so plentiful on Devil's Elbow. If the PCs can control the majority of the stuff, they are in a position to pick and choose which among Riddleport's leaders gain access to the metal—if they choose to keep it all for themselves, several crimelords may take it upon themselves to send thugs, thieves, and even assassins against the PCs in an attempt to gain control of the metal for themselves.

Rescue the Prospectors: Each group of prospectors the PCs aid in returning to Riddleport earns them the gratitude of that group. For rescuing any number of cyphermages, the PCs are each granted a magic item worth no more than 2,000 gp from the Order's stores. For rescuing Goldhammer's dwarves, the Gas Forge offers to craft noqual weapons or armor for the PCs at greatly reduced prices (effectively negating the additional cost for creating the item out of noqual), although the amount of items they can create is limited to the amount of noqual the PCs can supply. Zincher begrudgingly gives the party a reward of 5,000 gp in pearls and gems if they help him escape the drows' influence and get back to Riddleport. Alas, there's nothing that can be done for Slyeg's doomed men—but if Slyeg can find a way to blame Zincher or the PCs for their fate, he certainly will do so.

If the Drow Escape: Of course, it's also possible for the PCs to simply take too long to get to the drow. How long it takes for the drow to complete their final days of research depends on you, but once Zincher and his men have captured at least six akatas (possibly with the PCs' help), Shindiira orders her charmed minion to have the captured creatures transported down to the piers at area **A.** That evening, a long, sleek ship of elven design sails into port—this is a swift elven warship called *Savahara,* one of many elven words for "swift and silent." *Savahara* is a ship the drow captured and used to come unseen under cover of night to Devil's Elbow in the first place, and unless the PCs intervene, they load their akatas, noqual, and any surviving drow onto the ship and set sail for the northwestern shores where the Mierani Forest meets the sea. In this case, the PCs might face the drow NPCs of this adventure in the next one, along with a large number of akatas and void zombies.

Into the Black

Just as no man is an island, no planet can exist entirely on its own. For many campaigns, it's enough to know that your adventurers conduct their acts of heroism and avarice against a backdrop of sun, moon, and stars. But for those who desire more information, whether to take their campaign off-world or merely to widen the scope of what might be at stake in an adventure, the following article provides a quick overview of the worlds beyond Golarion, and how they interact with your PCs' home.

THE SOLAR SYSTEM

Golarion, the planet on which most of the action in the Pathfinder Chronicles Campaign Setting takes place, is only one of 11 planets in its solar system (some of which have moons as large as Golarion itself, making the actual number of "worlds" much higher). Though not all of these worlds are inhabited, and some are host to climates and conditions so extreme as to be inhospitable to humanoid life, those who manage to break Golarion's bounds and travel to the stars are treated to wonders beyond anything their homeworld has to offer. Below are all the major bodies of Golarion's solar system, presented in order of their distance from the center.

The Sun: Given countless names, this mid-sized star is the source of all life across its surrounding solar system. Thousands of times larger than the planets that draw nourishment from it, the sun is a harsh and forbidding place, its incredible temperatures capable of destroying all but the most powerfully girded travelers. Still, some legends hold that even this impossibly huge floating furnace is inhabited, its vast surface populated by joyous creatures of flame and energy that roll and dive in its seas of celestial fire.

Since the beginning, the conscious races have looked to the sky for guidance. In the movements of the heavens, they seek meaning; in their positions, portents. The opulent halls of royal houses across Golarion play host to learned astrologers and scholars paid to interpret the songs of the spheres, and many are the battlefields where chieftains on both sides offer bloody sacrifice to the red planet Akiton. Varisians follow the motions of their Cosmic Caravan, and all followers of Desna pay special attention to her children, who light the night sky and guide sailors to their moorage. Though some may scoff at those who deify Golarion's sister worlds, few gazing upon the great crater of the Inner Sea can deny the sky's power when riled.

All men watch the stars. Yet how many know that the stars gaze back at them?

—Greogorik Taraspi,
Chief Astrological Advisor to the court of Xerbystes II

Aballon, the Horse: Named for the speed with which it races across the sky, Aballon is the closest planet to its mother star. So close is its orbit, in fact, that its surface is a charred and rocky wasteland, its sands bleached white or burned black and in some places forming vast seas of glass. Yet while its desolate surface and temperatures capable of melting lead provide ample explanation for the planet's lack of inhabitation, such was obviously not always the case. Here and there across the landscape, the jagged, needle-like spires of ruined cities protrude from the shifting sands. Who built them and why they were abandoned remains unknown, but scholars speculate that some particularly hardy race—perhaps elemental or mechanical in nature—might have settled here in order to harness as much of the sun's energy as possible.

Castrovel, the Green: Much as the red planet Akiton has traditionally been associated with war, Golarion's closest neighbor, Castrovel, has long been looked upon as the celestial home of lust and fertility—and with good reason. Within its lush, steamy jungles, strange primeval swamps, and oceans of colored mist, the green planet is ruled by some of the most stunning creatures in the system. Humanoid in form, the Lashunta are an educated, civilized matriarchal society. From the backs of their terrible lizard steeds, the breathtakingly beautiful women of the Lashunta city-states maneuver for political position while banding together to keep the hordes of dangerous fauna away from their settlements. Ironically, while the females of the species resemble antennaed versions of ideal human women, their men are proportionally ugly. Barely half the height of their female counterparts and twice as broad, the rugged men of Castrovel are hairy and fierce, their prowess in battle matched only by their keen intellect and thirst for knowledge. Both sexes see the pursuit of mental perfection, the unlocking of the brain's utmost potential, as the most noble of goals, and as a result Castrovel is a fertile breeding ground for psions and telepaths.

Golarion: This verdant planet is the primary focus of the Pathfinder Chronicles Campaign Setting. It has a single moon, which is tidally locked so as to constantly show the same face to its parent planet. While that face is barren and gray, a world obviously bereft of life, some whisper that its desolation is merely an elaborate ploy, and that life lurks just beyond the horizon, avoiding the prying eyes of terrestrial astronomers.

Akiton, the Red: Colder and harder than Golarion, Akiton is a planet of brave four-armed warriors, their lances and flechette rifles gleaming against a backdrop of rust-red rock and sand. Monsters roam these cold mountains and desolate plains, and tyrannical empires raise stark and beautiful cities in the dried beds of ancient oceans. The tribes of the Shobhad-neh, 12-foot-tall behemoths capable of wielding a sword in each of their four hands, are fiercely territorial, and few sane creatures would challenge a single warrior girded in his battle harness, let alone one of the warbands and raiding parties that constantly redraw the giants' borders. Yet there are other races here as well: the timid and crafty Ysoki rat-men, or the red-skinned lizardfolk who hunt the great sand serpents with only crude spears and teeth. Perhaps strangest of all are the Contemplatives of Ashok, into whose soft and throbbing brain-sacs the ether occasionally whispers secrets of things past and those left to come.

Verces, the Line: This inhospitable world draws its name from the fact that it is tidally locked, with the same hemisphere always facing the sun. With one side of the planet baking in the constant radiation that punches through its thin atmosphere and the other losing its heat into the darkness to space, civilization on Verces is confined exclusively to a narrow band circling the planet on the terminator, the line where night meets day. Here, however, its humanoid residents have compensated by building enormous linked settlements, their towering

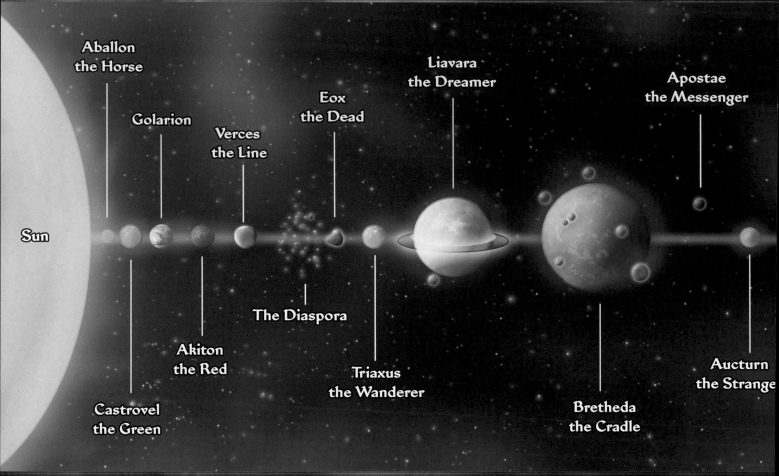

palaces ringing the planet in gleaming metal and artificial light. When required to venture into either Darkside or the Fullbright, as they frequently must in order to hunt the bizarre creatures who live there or to mine the crystals that power their monolithic factories, residents of Verces wear bulky protective suits that are a synthesis of magic and machine, protecting them from heat and cold and frequently enhancing their physical and combat abilities.

The Diaspora: This solar system did not always have 11 planets. Once, long before the men of Golarion began to write down their histories, there were 13 great worlds circling the sun. What caused the destruction of two planets is unknown—perhaps a war between neighboring worlds, a shift in orbits leading to a collision, or an encounter with some terror from the space between the stars. All that is certain is that where once two living worlds dwelt, there is now only the Diaspora. Occasionally known by other names, such as the March of Stars, this thick asteroid belt is rife with both destruction and life. Despite regular (on an astronomical scale) collisions with each other, the countless tumbling rocks and dwarf planets in this field play host to numerous tiny worlds and fiefdoms, from single miles-wide asteroids claimed by individual wizards seeking solitude to debris large

enough to hold their own atmospheres and seas of liquid water, squabbled over intensely by the creatures who make the field their home. In this tumult, great long-legged spider creatures launch themselves from rock to rock with a mathematical precision, foraging for mineral deposits, while pale angelic beings soar through the field on moth wings of pure energy, riding the solar wind.

Eox, the Dead: For generations, various cultures on Golarion have sensed that there's something wrong with the dim planet of Eox, seeing in its retrograde orbit strange and sinister omens. If only they knew how right they were—for Eox is a dead world in the most literal sense. Once the alien race most similar to humanity in physiology, the men of Eox were some of the most accomplished magic users in the solar system, a people known for their extraordinary ability to bend space and time. Constantly striving for new discoveries, they pushed themselves hard, sacrificing aesthetics, love, and morality in their pursuit of power—some say that they even managed to ascend to godhood and form their own pantheon. But whether it was a punishment by the deities for their hubris, a weapon from an unknown enemy, or merely an arcane experiment gone terribly wrong, Eox's shining age of reason ended in a single white-hot moment. So powerful was that world-ending explosion that it set Eox's very atmosphere aflame, burning off the gasses in a planet-wide firestorm.

Most of the populace was killed instantly, but for those few who survived in self-contained environments, it was the beginning of a new era. With no atmosphere to breathe, a critically low population, and many of their people sterilized by the vast wash of radiation, the remaining inhabitants of Eox turned to undeath, permanently capping their population. In the millennia since, the bone sages of Eox have grown wiser, more powerful, and even less bound by morality, concerned only with the one pursuit left to them: magic. While nothing is certain, it's whispered that the denizens of the blasted planet may have had something to do with the formation of the Diaspora.

Triaxus, the Wanderer: In many ways, Triaxus is actually two worlds. Dubbed "the Wanderer" due to its extremely eccentric orbit, Triaxus's distance from the system's center varies greatly as it traces its slow, elliptical path around the sun. At its farthest point, out near the great gas giants, the sun is a mere pinpoint, and the world is one of glaciers and vast snowfields. At its closest point, however, Triaxus is even closer to the sun than steamy Castrovel. What is most amazing about this annual change is that Triaxus bears life—is, in fact, flush with it—and plays home to two distinct ecologies, each of which goes dormant while the other is ascendant. During the Triaxian winter, the civilized people of the planet hunker down in towns and castles made of ice and stone, hunting the giant furred insects and terrifying snowbirds of the plains while burning pale fungi for warmth. In the summer, the glaciers melt and recede in great monsoons, and the people abandon their stalwart forts to live free and easy in the jungles that spring up overnight, feeding off the plentiful wildlife. Given that one complete cycle on Triaxus takes hundreds of Golarion years to complete, yet their people rarely live more than 80 years, Triaxian society is a strange and awkward thing, with those generations born into the fertile times toiling to prepare for a season of hardship they know only from legends and may never live to see.

Liavara, the Dreamer: One of the solar system's two titanic gas giants, Liavara is easily recognizable by its bright rings, great fields of charged dust that play host to a surprising variety of strange and tiny elemental beings. In addition, the heavy gases that make up the planet's outer layers brim with a number of amorphous and gliding monsters, some of which are believed to have been brought to the planet by Brethedan explorers who then went feral themselves, becoming just another part of the planet's buoyant ecosystem. (Though their language is difficult to parse into human terms, the highest-evolved inhabitants of Liavara are called "dreamers" by

ELVES AND SOVYRIAN

While everyone who knows the story of the elves' exodus and eventual return to Golarion has likely heard the name Sovyrian, few members of other races know anything solid about the secret realm of the elves. Most believe it to be on another world, though whether the elves originated there and traveled to Golarion in the distant past or are native to Golarion and discovered their hidden realm later on is a subject hotly debated. Although those select few who have traveled to Sovyrian via Kyonin's mysterious gate, the *Sovyrian Stone*, are notoriously tight-lipped about it, the land is rumored to be a place of strange and ethereal beauty, with tall spires and delicate domes—certainly the embodiment of elven aesthetics, if not the birthplace. Indeed, it should be noted that only the demon Treerazer's attempt to pervert the gateway between the worlds was sufficient to draw the elves back to Golarion after milennia in their secret abode. Why they decided to stay once that threat was dealt with remains a mystery. For now, however, the elves seem content to retake their ancestral holdings and entrench themselves once more as one of the ruling races of Golarion—though none can say when they might suddenly decide to emigrate once again.

their Brethedan counterparts, and appear to be held in considerable esteem.)

The true civilization on Liavara exists on its several sizable moons, most important of which is Arkanen. This well-populated moon is in a strange position, as on its own it seems unable to successfully hold its atmosphere and constantly bleeds off its air into the surrounding space in a white, comet-like tail. Once a year, however, the moon's orbit around Liavara takes it so close that it actually plunges through the upper layers of the giant's atmosphere, tearing away enough gas to keep its ecosystem functional for another year. As vital as this annual refueling is to sustaining life on Arkanen, it's also an extremely dangerous time—catastrophic storms wrack the moon, predators from Liavara's upper atmosphere sometime sail between worlds, and great bolts of lightning caused by disruptions in the worlds' magnetic fields arc between the two. This last phenomenon is a source of great power for the wizards and scientists of Arkanen, and most major projects take place at this time of year. Strangely enough, conventional physics holds that Arkanen's orbit and theft of gas from the giant should be impossible, supporting the theory that the moon may have been created magically as a sort of arcane dynamo in order to power some unknown undertaking.

Bretheda, the Cradle: The largest planet in the system, the Cradle takes its name from the fact that

CONSTELLATIONS

While the information presented here focuses primarily on Golarion's sister worlds and the cultures that inhabit them, the stars themselves have considerable impact on the societies of Golarion. From Cynosure, the immobile northern star which allows travelers to navigate and houses Desna's celestial palace, to the 13 signs of the Cosmic Caravan which offer portents to astrologers, the stars are revered by priests and atheists alike, and are even worshiped outright by some. One of the various ways in which civilizations interact with the stars is through the creation and propagation of constellations. Presented below are twenty of the more commonly recognized star-pictures, along with their most prevalent associations.

Ardacondis: Who wrestles the Kraken to keep it from choking the world.

The Caravan: Which protects all who travel.

The Fang: That vampires kill for.

The Ferryman: Who claims lost souls.

The Gecko: Who climbed up to the sky.

Gigas Major: The old giant.

Gigas Minor: The young giant.

The Hawk: Who hunts the heavens and defends the sun.

The Key: That Abadar made to unlock the First Vault.

The Kraken: Who ensnares Ardacondis.

The Owl King: Who watches everything in the night.

The Sea Wraith: The notorious vessel of Besmara, the Pirate Queen.

The Sorcerer: Who all spellcasters honor and look to for guidance.

The Sphinx: Who knows many secret things, and whom even the gods respect.

The Spider: Who weaves the night in its silken strands.

The Stair of Stars: The pathway that leads the faithful to Desna's palace of Cynosure.

The Stirge: Whose nose got stuck in the sky.

The Tarrasque: Who sleeps among the stars for now, but will return when the time comes to end the world.

The Throne: Reserved for the final king.

The Wyrm: The great star-dragon, considered good by some and evil by others, who guards his celestial hoard.

it plays mother to literally dozens of moons, many of them inhabited. On the planet itself, the vast seas of blue and purple clouds shelter a far-reaching and highly intelligent society, though perhaps the one most alien to human thought and seemingly bereft of conventional technology. To the Brethedans (called "floaters" by some), the proper response to any problem is evolution. Drifting like enormous, contented blimps, the jellyfish-like aliens possess a rough but highly creative hive mind and an incredible ability to adapt their bodies consciously, allowing them to bind together to meet threats or harden themselves against the vacuum of space in order to visit other worlds.

Bretheda's moons are almost a solar system of their own, and so numerous that new ones are still being discovered by astronomers. Of considerable prominence is Kalo-Mahoi—an ocean world with a thick ice crust, beneath which its people build beautiful and delicate cities along its deep-sea geothermal vents—but there are numerous other moons just as interesting. Some of these include Varos, a violently volcanic world that is heated tidally as the gas giant's gravity distorts its shape; Dykon, a crystalline world on which silicon-based life thrives in bright, sharp-edged forests; or Thyst, where massive radioactivity is the lifeblood of its natives and certain death for unwary visitors.

Apostae, the Messenger: This tiny, rocky world operates well out of the plane of the ecliptic in an orbit nearly perpendicular to Golarion's own, with its strange course suggesting that it may have formed elsewhere and been captured later by the sun's gravity well. Adding to the mystery of its origin are the great miles-wide metal doors set flush with its barren surface in several places. Ornate and covered in strange symbols, these doors make it unclear whether the planet is in fact inhabited by a race of subterranean creatures, or perhaps even some sort of vessel from somewhere beyond the solar system. Among those who know of its questionable origin, a prevalent theory proposes that this strange object may even have brought the first spark of life to Golarion's system, but such claims can only be dismissed as fancy until someone passes through the magically warded doors and into whatever waits below.

Aucturn, the Stranger: Most astronomers in Golarion's system would prefer to forget that Aucturn exists, so inimical is it to their scientific methods. Unreachable by all but the most powerful magic, and the only world in the system not connected to other planets by a network of portals, Aucturn is the subject of countless legends. A world of monsters, say some, or the home of an ancient god woken at last from a million years of dark slumber. Certainly there are hints that the planet may be the system's link to the lightless places between the stars known as the Dark Tapestry, or to the mysterious Dominion of the Black whispered about in Osiriani legend. Perhaps it exists in a slightly different dimension, a link between this and another universe. No one can say for sure, but for thousands of years it has unnerved astronomers who, peering at it through their telescopes and scrying spells, all report very different descriptions, from a terrestrial world with atmosphere to a ringed gas giant to a dark and lifeless rock—even when observing it through the same shared telescope.

TRAVELING BETWEEN WORLDS

Though there may seem to be an astonishing amount of life squeezed into Golarion's solar system, the distances between these planets is so vast as to be almost unimaginable. Only magic of the highest possible caliber, or technology far beyond that which is known to most civilizations on Golarion, is capable of bridging the gap between worlds, and those few who might be privy to such methods grasp their secrets tightly. Yet exceptions remain, and three of the most accessible methods of interplanetary travel are presented here.

Portals

Almost all those who live on Golarion have heard the story of the great elf exodus before the fall of the *Starstone*, the way the entirety of elven society marched silently through magical stone portals to gather in Kyonin, there to step through a final arch and disappear from the world for millennia, transported to the mysterious haven known as Sovyrian. Few realize, however, that these portals far predate the elves' existence on Golarion and may be the inspiration for the race's fabled *elfgates*. These profoundly ancient passages form a vast network linking all the system's planets save Aucturn (one reason why the learned fear and distrust the dark planet). The knowledge of how to operate these ancient artifacts is rare on Golarion, and in fact remains so across the system, though the warrior-scholars of Castrovel learned long ago how to use the portals to step between their own world and the red planet of Akiton, giving those two worlds the most contact of any in the system. In recent years, however, portals across the system have begun winking on seemingly at random, activating for brief stretches of time and offering those nearby a glimpse through a window into another world—or, for those brave or foolish enough, a doorway.

Who built these portals remains a mystery, but it's possible they left a clue behind. A strange portal on Apostae, similar in shape to the others but with wildly different markings, has so far not been connected to any other known portals, leading those most informed about such things to believe that the architects of the portals may have originated far outside the solar system and left this as a link, waiting for the young races here to mature enough to decipher its operation and make contact.

Spells

While many believe that spells such as *greater teleport* have no limit to their range, those who have tried to use them to reach the stars know otherwise. Some attribute it to the mind's inability to truly comprehend the distances involved, others to the great speed with which the celestial bodies move through the blackness, and still others to the lack of any sort of ether for the magic to travel through. Whatever the cause, most have concluded that it's easier to shift planes and explore the universe's mysteries that way than to travel across spaces so vast. Conventional

scrying methods are likewise inhibited by the incredible distance. Still, for those determined enough, magic can sometimes do the job via spells (see page 54) or through the construction of massive and convoluted artifacts, some of which can still occasionally be found abandoned by their creators on planets like Golarion.

Vessels

By far the most terrifying and dangerous means of interplanetary travel is through the use of starships. Over the lifespan of the solar system, several cultures have tried to build vessels capable of spanning the cold distances between worlds, and a few have succeeded. The great metal dirigibles of Verces, for instance, have set sail from their needle-like space elevators and explored the Diaspora numerous times, observing the myriad life forms there through their thick portholes. The bone

Cayden Cailean

Cayden Cailean (CAY-den CAY-lee-en) is one of the Ascended, a mortal man who became a god after passing the grueling tests of the magical *Starstone*. Legend tells that, unlike the other Ascended, he was completely drunk at the time and attempted the test on a dare from another drunk. Three days after entering the Cathedral of the Starstone, he emerged a living god, baffled and amused about what the Test might have entailed. A good-natured sellsword as a mortal, his behavior changed little as a god, and he continued to fight for just causes, sample various drinks, and avoid things he didn't want to do. Thus, Cayden Cailean became the patron of brave men, alcoholic spirits, and freedom to choose your own path in life.

Cayden Cailean is outgoing, friendly, boisterous, unashamed, and flirtatious, even more so when he allows himself to indulge in fermented delights. He loves good-spirited toasts, friendly bar brawls, bawdy songs, and standing up for the underdog. He loathes slavery, mean-spiritedness, bullying, teetotalers, and restrictive laws and customs. He believes that everyone would get along better if they could sit down and have a drink, preferably in the company of lovely ladies. A former mercenary, he believes in fair pay for a job well done, whether paid in coin, drink, or a tumble in the hay with a willing paramour. Having had his share of hard times as a mortal, he's not above helping someone for free now and then or leaving an extra-generous tip for someone in need. This simple and welcoming philosophy makes him popular with adventurers, philanthropists, revelers, and those who fight for good.

Although he is a god of wine, his interest is in merriment rather than forgetting old sorrows, whether that merriment is common folk at an alehouse or wealthy merchants sipping brandy at a feast. Likewise he is not fond of those who use drinking to work up enough courage (or whittle away enough wisdom) to bring harm upon others. He has been known to inspire tipsy revelers to speak insightful poetry and confess secrets better aired out than kept in the dark. It is traditional to toast his name with the first drink of the evening. A "Cayden's dare" is any foolish-seeming thing that turns out to have good consequences, such as going out to tip the mayor's cow and discovering a discarded pouch of coins or going on a quest the night before your mother-in-law comes to visit. At weddings it is common to joke that the bride or groom is only present because of a drunken dare.

Cayden Cailean was a courageous man, although often his courage was bolstered by a wineskin or flask. He expects his followers to be brave in the face of danger, though there is no shame in retreat; he is the god of bravery, not reckless stupidity in the face of common sense. Although many assume his faithful will accept any dare in the name of bravery, the truth is that they are not routinely foolish just because of their religion. Even the dullest hero of Cayden Cailean has the sense to not accept an impossible or suicidal challenge—though it is not uncommon to accept a risky one after a swig or two of "liquid courage."

"Don't let rules get in the way of enjoying what is truly good in life."
—Placard of Wisdom, line 1

Although his other divine concerns are flexible in interpretation, he is as hard as a nail when it comes to a person's right to freedom. Before the Test of the Starstone he had been known to leave in the middle of mercenary jobs when he found out his employer was a tyrant or using him to bring harm to decent folk, which (coupled with his drinking) gave him a somewhat unreliable reputation, but he refused to go against his own beliefs for the sake of mere coin. Cayden Cailean believes that there is no justice in a law that oppresses one man to benefit another, and over the centuries he has worked to counter the plots of lawful deities who see human misery as a price to pay in the name of some goal. He has been known to kill slavers, or (in lands where slavery is legal) buy slaves, free them, and then later rob the slave owner so there would be no profit in the slaving. In places where the peasantry suffers from harsh taxes or demoralizing practices such as *primae noctis*, he has helped them topple their oppressor or at least aided them in escaping to more friendly lands. Of course, he is still good and doesn't believe that you should be able to murder your neighbors even though the law forbids it, nor is he a destructive god of chaos or a madcap god of frivolity.

Most of his worshipers are common folk who seek simple contentment in their daily lives, have a drink with their friends, and have the courage to stand up to evil when it rears its ugly head, no matter what shape it is in. Brewers, vintners, barkeeps, and innkeepers pray to him for tasty beverages and the good business that comes from them. Happy drunks and revelers of all sorts toast his name. Wealthy folk do good deeds in honor of him, like simply sharing a private store of wine in lean times. Cayden Cailean is a very popular deity among good adventurers, who share his casual goals of questing and celebrating one's victories. Those not keen on adventuring often work as guides or explorers, enjoying the freedom of living and going wherever they please. His followers are happy people, preferring to look on the bright side of things and accepting any downturn as a challenge to make right. While most of his worshipers are human, a significant number are half-elves, finding comfort and acceptance in a faith interested in good works and good times rather than formal hierarchies, ancient traditions, and old grudges. Although dwarves appreciate his interest in ale, few worship him, though some clans will lift a mug in his name and include him in stories about Torag, where he typically takes the role of a humorous sidekick.

Cayden Cailean's direct intervention in the mortal world isn't frequent, but he has been known to prevent a keg from emptying (often to convince good folk to congregate a little longer in a place of safety) or push someone especially meek to gain a backbone of hardened steel at a key time. Those who go against his simple tenets may find themselves ill the next time they drink, intoxicated when clarity is needed, or frightened by common animals or shadows. When he is happy, drinks are more savory, the night air feels more brisk and smells more sweet, and courage burns white-hot.

Cayden Cailean's image is much as he looked in life: an average-looking bronze-skinned human with a tankard in one hand, and often wearing chainmail. In grander art, he is sometimes shown fending off a swarm of devils with his well-worn rapier, all the while his tankard held high. In a few places, he is sometimes shown with broken shackles hanging loosely from his wrists representing breaking free of mortal concerns, and in areas where his faith has brought freedom from oppression or slavery, they interpret the shackles more literally.

Formal raiment of a Cayden Cailean priest is a simple brown tunic or robe with a wine-red stole bearing the god's ale-mug symbol. As he cares little for finery and ostentation, ceremonial objects in a temple are primarily functional rather than decorative, and a high priest of Cayden Cailean would think nothing of performing a blessing with water or wine from a common bar mug rather than a bejeweled font. His church's holy water may be blessed water, wine, ale, or other spirits, though the stuff intended for use against evil monsters is usually of inferior quality. After all, why waste good wine by throwing it at something?

It is interesting to note that Cayden Cailean is the only major god who uses a surname. In his early years as a god, he insisted that his last name be included in all forms of address, an unusual habit for someone normally so relaxed about formalities. The prevalent opinions on the matter are that he wished to distance himself from another mortal named Cayden (perhaps someone of evil intent) or honor his parents who might have died when he was young. This second theory is corroborated by his interest in sponsoring orphanages, perhaps as a thank-you to the long-gone orphanage that raised him. Cayden ignores questions about it, insisting it was decided long ago and there are more important things to talk about.

There are many mortals alive today with the surname Cailean, and they may be distantly related to the god, but the issue is muddled because it is common for children raised in orphanages funded by the church to take the god's surname as their own when they leave. Thus, the handsome farmhand might be a direct descendant of Cayden Cailean's brother or merely the grown-up survivor of a goblin attack that wiped out entire families.

Cayden Cailean is chaotic good, and his portfolio is freedom, alcohol, and bravery. His domains are Chaos, Charm, Good, Strength, and Travel, and his favored weapon is the rapier. His holy symbol is a tankard of ale, with or without a rich head of foam on it. Most of his clergy are clerics, with a handful of druids who attend to sacred vineyards and small patches of barley and hops for brewing small quantities of famous tasty ales. Some bards of the faith consider themselves part of the clergy, numbering at most five percent of the number of priests, but using their music to entertain, inspire, and mend those they meet. Cayden Cailean has few adepts, no more than the number of bards, and they usually reside in the most uncivilized areas, often just a hermit wanting to be left alone to enjoy his little piece of the world. Cayden Cailean is called the Drunken Hero, the Lucky Drunk, and many other localized affectionate nicknames.

Services to Cayden Cailean always include a toast or a song. As the faith is not inclined to hold to formalities, a simple toast at a wedding might become a game of "dueling dares" between the groomsmen, and an official church holiday often resembles a festival more than a time of worship. Songs dedicated to Cayden Cailean typically involve shouting choruses, stomping feet, and the clanking of drinkware. Services may be indoors or outdoors, aboveground or below, day or night—whatever is appropriate to the occasion.

Cayden's church essentially has no hierarchy, as none of his priests really like other people telling them what to do, despite any good intentions. Elderly priests and those renowned as local heroes often garner special respect, but few attempt to lead by warrant of their age or reputations. Because of this lack of a central authority, the god himself sometimes has to send visions or dreams to his priests to encourage them to meet on an issue and decide on a plan of action. Most priests believe that problems are best dealt with by the people who discovered them and they don't bother trying to follow a chain of command unless a problem turns out to be too big to handle alone. The majority of the god's clergy are friendly with each other, and while there can be personal rivalries, those aren't anything that can't be solved with a bar fight.

TEMPLES AND SHRINES

The Drunken Hero has few buildings that function only as temples. Most of his sacred (to use that term lightly) buildings are just alehouses run by clergy members or small inns bearing a shrine to him above the bar. A rare few have additional decorations signifying their roles as temples, typically banners and high shelves stacked with empty wine bottles. Several large family breweries contain a small room set aside for the church, often staffed by a family member who enters the priesthood to secure prosperity for the brewery. In cities, the occasional feast hall might bear the symbol of Cayden Cailean on its sign or over its doors. These larger "temples" donate much of their earnings to promote the public good, ease the burden of the poor, or to fund pious adventurers.

Cayden's holy places are not thought of as houses of healing, and the casual nature of the faith means that a typical temple or shrine might only have a very low-level cleric on hand. If someone comes knocking covered in blood, the cleric will help just as any good cleric would, but most temples are also taverns and there is a business mentality in those working there. Anyone who receives help gets a cold eye if they leave without paying or at least buying a round for the house.

A CLERIC'S ROLE

Cayden Cailean's easygoing nature and lack of a central church agency mean that his clerics are able to use their discretion when it comes to how to advance his cause in the world. Some are solo crusaders for good, some found adventuring companies or support border towns in need of faith and comfort. Some brew ale or beer, some make wine,

> ## HOLY TEXT
>
> Although Cayden Cailean sees the use of writing and greatly enjoys written stories and poetry, his faith has but a single widely circulated holy text. Stories said to be favorites of the god of bravery receive wide circulation among members of his faith, however.
>
> **Placard of Wisdom:** Cayden rarely spent enough time in one place to read a book, let alone write one, and he prefers to keep his message simple. His simple holy text is known as the *Placard of Wisdom*, condensing his divine philosophy into a few short phrases suitable for hanging on the wall. Though the specific wording might vary from city to city or even from tavern to tavern, the general message is "do good, enjoy life, have a drink now and then, and stand up for what you believe in," easy words of common sense that appeal to all.

some plant crops for these beverages, and some involve themselves in the transport or sale of spirits. Some work with new communities or where there is poor sanitation to educate people on the health benefits of drinking ale and wine rather than common water, especially when herbal or magical disease treatments are scarce—extolling towns where ale or wine is commonly drunk as having fewer deaths from certain diseases than those that shun "Cayden's drink." City-based clerics might be heavily involved with the local brewers' or vintners' guild, oversee the quality of spirits for the city government, and so on. In smaller communities, a cleric might work as a mediator, teach farmers how to brew their own drinks in small quantities, and encourage townsfolk to share with their neighbors to create bonds of friendship. Explorer clerics and travelers in distant lands often look for new stories, rumors, and recipes to share, seek to assuage or combat the burden of slavery, and even scatter barley and grape seeds in the hopes of finding new places suitable for these crops.

Because of the god's close association with alcoholic beverages, clerics tend to have a high alcohol tolerance. Most individuals who are easily sickened from drinking or dislike the taste of alcohol usually do not enter the clergy, but the faith would never turn away a worthy potential who has no taste for booze.

The church is aware that some folk drink to the extent that it becomes a crutch or a poison to the will. Cayden Cailean and his priests believe this is a corruption and abuse of his favorite things, and sometimes a cleric takes it upon himself to counsel these poor souls, often using minor magic to bolster a patient's resolve and steering the person toward activities or work that improves the patient's life and negates the need to drown his sorrows.

Cleric explorers carry a small keg of strong ale or wine (which they might dilute with water, depending on the custom of their home city), and it is customary to ask a cleric to toast a blessing at any gathering of strangers (such as at a roadside inn). By custom, most brigands allow a cleric of Cayden Cailean to pass safely in exchange for a drink and a blessing, though this courtesy rarely extends to a cleric's companions.

The clergy has a tradition of drinking contests and "dueling dares" or boasting contests, all in good fun and never with the intent to harm or humiliate another. In a duel of dares, it is acceptable to refuse an outrageous or unreasonable dare, and in cases where contests become heated offering an outrageous dare presents a way for both participants to save face—in essence, the maker of the dare deliberately suggests something dangerous or impossible, giving the other player the option to refuse. The easiest way to do this is to suggest the other person take the Test of the Starstone, at which point the opponent usually says, "I am great, but not so great as Cayden Cailean," refusing the dare and buying the darer a drink in the hopes of becoming comrades.

A typical cleric of Cayden Cailean has at least one rank in a useful Craft or Profession skill. Most study Diplomacy, Gather Information, or Knowledge (geography or nature) to better influence people or enhance their craft. There is no official tithe but by friendly custom they tip well, especially at places owned by the church. They tend to have a more relaxed attitude about marriage than others in the community but develop close friendships with both sexes. Given Cayden Cailean's tendencies to "plough a furrow" in every town he visited, the temple-taverns often have younglings born of various traveling priests. They are raised by the church community, though parents are still held responsible for their children's welfare.

A typical day for a cleric involves waking, a prayer-toast, breakfast, and a period of work. Lunch and dinner are begun with a toast; in some places there is also a customary late afternoon drink of a hearty, thick ale. Evening is for friends, family, telling stories, and personal interests. Spell preparation takes place after breakfast.

The church uses no formal titles, though those who have a title from a guild or profession normally use that within the church as well.

A BARD'S ROLE

While many bards claim Cayden Cailean as their patron, only a small number are so devout that they consider themselves part of the clergy. At best, there's one such bard for every twenty clerics of the faith. Despite their use of arcane magic rather than divine, bards make remarkably good priests of the Drunken Hero: They have healing magic, are good with people, can inspire courage in the most timid heart, and are a welcome guest at any inn or tavern. Bards are proud to point out that it was their forebears who first spread the news of Cayden Cailean's ascension, the only person in nearly a thousand years to succeed at the Test of the Starstone, and bards believe that they (as a profession) have a dear place in the god's heart because of this. Their skills and magic make them excellent rabble-rousers in unhappy lands, and they like to keep an ear to the ground for such opportunities. Unlike clerics, they do not tend to carry small kegs, but otherwise they function in the church and larger society very similar to clerics.

THREE MYTHS

As well-told stories bring people together and speed travels like little else, Cayden Cailean's worshipers are very fond of legends, rumors, romances, and tales of epic adventure. Of particular popularity are such tales that have to do with the innumerable exploits of their deity—as both a god and as a man.

The Ballad of Salicotal's Fall: A few hundred years after Cayden Cailean's ascension, a powerful duke of Hell named Salicotal grew concerned with the young god's popularity, especially as it threatened his own interests in the temptations of wine. A wise, cultured devil with interests in lore and alchemy, Salicotal challenged Cayden to a duel to the death to take place on neutral ground and be judged by Pharasma. The god replied with a challenge of his own, a game of "dueling dares," and if Cayden lost he would submit to Salicotal's spear. The fiend agreed and the two met. One by one they escalated their dares, Salicotal's clever and risky, Cayden's courageous and subtly insulting, with the young god taking a swig of his finest brew after each. Eventually the devil grew so angry at the insults that he attacked. Thinking they were equally matched at fisticuffs, the fiend charged, but Cayden tore off Salicotal's wings and beat him to death with them, sending the devil's spirit back to Hell greatly diminished. Flushed from victory and drink, Cayden continued his rise in popularity, and he used the devil's wing bones to create devil-slaying crossbow bolts for his greatest followers.

Finding of the Cayhound: Cayden's most trusted companion as a mortal was his mastiff, Thunder. Two years before his ascension, Cayden found a litter of pups huddled near their scrawny mother who had just died. Despite their hunger and fear of a stranger, the pups growled at him and stood guard over their dead mother. Amazed at the courage in such tiny creatures, he offered them food, befriended them, buried their mother, and took them home to raise them. He gave five of the pups to friends and family and kept the largest for himself, whom he named Thunder for his deep growls. Thunder guarded Cayden's home while he was away, and the dog disappeared shortly after the ascension, joining the god in Elysium. Not long after, several red-coated mastiffs were spotted in and around Absalom. These celestial riding dogs came to be known as cayhounds, the favored pets of Cayden Cailean.

The Thousand Songs of the Starstone: These varied tales offer theories about what dangers Cayden faced during the Test of the Starstone and explanations on how he bypassed or overcame them. Though a "thousand" is an exaggeration, there are at least one hundred popular versions of the tale, usually colored by local businesses, favorite drinks, and rivalries. Only fools believe the stories are true—after all, if the truth were known more would have passed the Test by now—but their purpose is to entertain, not educate. A worldly listener can often tell where a person was born and raised based on their version of the story, and traveling bards often use versions from far lands to entertain local crowds with the "strange beliefs" of foreigners.

HOLIDAYS

The church believes that every day is a reason to celebrate—life, good friends, good wine, and so on. They only acknowledge two holidays meriting extra festivities.

First Brewing: After the first harvest, a small amount is set aside to create ale, wine, or stronger drink. When this is ready for tasting, the community comes together to sample the first brewing of the year and toast Cayden's name. Because of local variables in the date of the harvest and different brewing times, this holiday has no set date but is normally about one month after harvest-time.

MAGIC OF CAYDEN CAILEAN

Clerics of Cayden Cailean may prepare *neutralize poison* as a 3rd-level spell. His clerics may also spontaneously cast *knock* as a 1st-level spell but only to open welds, shackles, or chains used to imprison or hobble someone (his bards may learn *knock* as if it were a 2nd-level spell on the bard spell list). Clerics' *create water* spell can create simple ale or wine (1 cup per level), and their *create food and water* spell can be used to make ale or wine rather than water (which spoils at the same rate the food does). Cayden Cailean's followers also have an additional spell only available to those of the faith, as described below.

DRUNKARD'S BREATH

School conjuration (creation); **Level** bard 2, cleric 2

EFFECT
Range 30 ft.
Area cone-shaped burst

DESCRIPTION
This spell emanates from your mouth and functions like *stinking cloud*, except as noted above. The effect is barely visible and does not obscure vision. The nausea effect resembles that of an extreme hangover. This is a poison effect. Cayden Cailean's church uses this spell to disperse angry crowds, such as when celebrations get out of hand.

Ascension Day: The actual date of Cayden's transformation from mortal to god is irrelevant even to him, but the church celebrates this event on the 11th of Kuthona with a toast of thanks to him for his gifts. Typically this is a hot alcoholic beverage with a sweet bread pastry of some kind.

APHORISMS

As many worshipers of Cayden Cailean are quick to swear, they often do so by their god's name.

In Cayden's Name: Flowery speeches are for bards, yet common warriors still need a poignant turn phrase, either to exclaim in the heat of battle or offer in honor of the dead. Before combat it is said as a toast, followed by a healthy swallow of Cayden's brew.

Sweet Barleybrew!: Usually uttered in surprise or amazement, whether at the sight of an approaching army, a taste of the brewmaster's best, or a peek at a barmaid's treasures. It can also call out unpleasant things, such as the taste of beer gone bad, the face of a half-orc, or the imminent arrival of the barmaid's father.

By the Light of the Starstone: Used both as an oath (on the rare times his followers swear serious oaths) and a declaration of something so profound that saying "sweet barleybrew!" proves insufficient. It is interesting to note that this phrase is used even though most people have no idea what the *Starstone* looks like or if it actually gives off light.

CHEVALIER

HIT DICE: D10

Class Level	Base Attack Bonus	Fort Save	Ref Save	Will Save	Special
1st	+1	+2	+0	+2	Aura of courage, recklessness
2nd	+2	+3	+1	+3	Controlled charge, stubborn mind
3rd	+3	+3	+1	+3	Poison immunity, smite evil

Skills (4 + Int bonus per level): Balance, Bluff, Craft, Diplomacy, Gather Information, Intimidate, Perform, Profession, Survival, Tumble.

RELATIONS WITH OTHER RELIGIONS

Cayden doesn't go out of his way to provoke fights with other godly beings but isn't afraid to take a few swings if challenged. He avoids evil deities unless they are directly causing trouble, at which point he is all battle cries and heroic charges and inspiring speeches followed by lightning-quick cuts of his blade. He is on very good terms with Desna, Sarenrae, and most especially Shelyn (whom he delights in serenading). He has been known to travel with Erastil, though the senior god can be a little too somber and dutiful for Cayden's tastes, and he and Torag like to meet and show off the latest human and dwarven brews. He is coolly friendly with Gozreh, for while his beloved drinks rely on nature's bounty, Gozreh is sometimes angry about wildlands being converted to cropland. He considers Irori too stuffy and Abadar tolerable but too forgiving of oppression in the name of progress. He occasionally trysts with Calistria but remains wary of her, there having been more than one bitter occasion in which the beauteous goddess of lust has gotten the best of him. Those who infer that Cayden only took the Test of the Starstone in an attempt to impress Calistria quickly find themselves on his bad side.

CHEVALIER

Some heroes don't believe in fancy rules or high creeds or big flowery speeches, they just want to kill evil things, spend time with friends, and swap great tales over a good meal and tasty drinks. Not as stuffy or restrictive as a full-fledged knighthood, in their hearts chevaliers are just good people who want to celebrate the good things in life and fight evil wherever it dares to tread.

Chevaliers welcome all like-minded folk regardless of religion, though most of them worship Cayden Cailean. Most are fighters, rogues, or barbarians, but sorcerers, clerics, and bards are not unheard of. Chevaliers often wear golden pins noting their patron liege or deity or the token of a lover or other whom they fight. Membership is easily obtained by swearing an oath in the presence of another chevalier and invoking the name of who they fight for or the figure that embodies their desire to do good in the world. An adventurer-turned-innkeeper in a frontier town, a band of travelers looking for bandits, and a would-be dragonslayer might all be chevaliers. They mix lofty intentions, unusual combat techniques, and stubborn determination into a strangely effective combination.

Requirements

To qualify to become a chevalier, a character must fulfill all of the following criteria:

Alignment: Good. Most are neutral good or chaotic good, with a rare few lawful good.

Base Attack Bonus: +6.

Skills: Gather Information 4 ranks, Knowledge (local) 4 ranks.

Special: A would-be chevalier must have succeeded at a challenge requiring great heroism; for example, they must participate in an encounter with an EL at least 3 levels greater than their level. (Being carried through an encounter by a group of more experienced heroes is not courageous.)

Class Features

The following are class features of the chevalier prestige class.

Aura of Courage (Su): A chevalier has an aura of courage like that of a 3rd-level paladin.

Recklessness (Ex): Sometimes hasty action proves more useful than even the best laid plans. A chevalier gains a morale bonus equal to his class level on attack and damage rolls on the round he enters a battle. A chevalier only gains this bonus against an opponent (or group of opponents) once per day. Thus, he cannot leave a battle and reengage moments later to gain the benefits of this ability more than once in the same battle.

Controlled Charge (Ex): At 2nd level, a chevalier no longer takes a –2 penalty to AC when charging.

Stubborn Mind (Ex): At 3rd level, a chevalier gains an incredibly stubborn determination. If he is affected by an enchantment spell or effect and fails his saving throw, he can attempt it again 1 round later at the same DC. He gets only this one extra chance to succeed on his saving throw (though this does not prevent him from using other means to break the effect, such as a rogue's slippery mind ability).

Poison Immunity (Ex): At 3rd level, a chevalier becomes immune to poison.

Smite Evil (Su): Once per day, a chevalier can smite evil as if he were a paladin of his character level.

NPC PRIESTS OF CAYDEN CAILEAN

Although countless people raise their voices in worship of Cayden Cailean, the god of bravery recognizes the truly faithful, distinguishing between the pious and mere revelers. PCs might encounter any of the following devout of Cayden Cailean during their travels.

Nemm Cailean (CG male human cleric 6) is broad-shouldered and scruffy but always has a pleasant grin on his face. He was raised in a church-sponsored orphanage and took the god's last name as his own, eventually joining the clergy. His goals are finding fame, fighting evil, and acquiring money to support other orphanages so more children can benefit from the church's generosity. He is personally offended by guilds that employ children as beggars or thieves and has been known to drag reluctant urchins to church or sponsor them into good families. This makes him unpopular with unscrupulous guilds, and he's been run out of town on more than one occasion.

Lorie the Cat (NG female half-elf cleric 1/rogue 8) is tall and wire-thin, with black hair and a large nose. Graceful and quiet, she enjoys dressing up and sneaking into fancy parties as a "mystery guest" so she can hear the latest gossip and sample the finest wines. She considers herself a "righteous assassin," targeting evil that the law ignores or cannot touch. She'll hire on for any good cause, always with an ear to the ground for something more important that requires her attention. She likes to laugh, duel, and has made men of many handsome farm boys. Her prized possession is a *ring of feather falling*, which she has used many times to evade pursuit or vengeful bodyguards.

Wellar the Fantastic (CN male human bard 1/cleric 1/fighter 1) is a boastful, friendly fellow with ruddy cheeks, fine blond hair, and a general look of awkwardness. He was a common sellsword until he met a priest of Cayden in Absalom and took to the faith like a drunk to a barrel. Inspired by tales of the god, he wants to become a great hero that bards will sing tales about, and to get things started he has learned to play a lute and compose his own songs (with only passable talent at either). Wellar has plenty of enthusiasm but no clear focus (partly because he drinks too much) and would benefit greatly from a mentor.

PLANAR ALLIES

Along with Thais, the Accidental Herald of Cayden Cailean (see page 86), and those creatures noted in the "Allies of Cayden Cailean" sidebar, the following beings

---

ALLIES OF CAYDEN CAILEAN

Cayden's priests can use *summon monster* spells to summon the following creatures in addition to those listed in the following spells..

SUMMON MONSTER II
Cayhound (celestial riding dog; CG)

SUMMON MONSTER III
Satyr, without pipes (CG)

SUMMON MONSTER V
Rust monster (N)
Satyr, with pipes (CG)

---

also serve the god of freedom and only answer *planar ally* and similar calling spells from his faithful.

Little Thunder: This Large celestial cayhound is one of Cayden Cailean's pet mastiff Thunder's favored sons. He speaks in a great booming voice, is quick to laugh, has a bawdy sense of humor, and is fond of strong beer. Once per day, he can growl at maximum volume, equivalent to a *shout* spell. Like his father he welcomes battle, but if innocents are in danger he strives to move them to safety first. He prefers kegs of ale or wine or even potions as payment for his services, as he has difficulty using other items.

Luthier, the Knight of the Vinyard: This man looks more like a fat minstrel than a knight, dressed in colorful leathers and carrying a mandolin and rapier. He also appears to be quite drunk, swaying with every step, mumbling half of his words, and frequently dropping his sword or instrument. Despite his appearance, he is a fearsome enemy of evil and cruelty, snapping to attention when the scent of blood is in the air and dancing across the battlefield with acrobatic grace. His leather armor is as hard as steel, his mandolin produces notes as clear as church bells, and his hands are as fast and dexterous as any pickpocket or wizard. Luthier is a half-celestial human bard 8/fighter 4. He loves fine wine and fine food, and those wishing to bargain for his services should have both on-hand for the discussion.

Valon, the Spirit of Spirits: This ghostlike creature is the friendly soul of a priest whose body was utterly destroyed long ago in a battle with evil. Knowledgeable in esoteric histories and obscure lore, he often held that beer was the greatest of any race's inventions. While he can manifest as an incorporeal creature, he prefers to possess the body of a willing humanoid (typically the cleric who calls him) as he misses the sensations of life, and he has been known to drink and carouse if the opportunity presents itself. If the cause is right, he is willing to serve in exchange for "a night on the town" in a borrowed body.

Teeth of Araska

South of the Arch of Aroden, near the everlasting hurricane known as the Eye of Abendego, the notorious pirate captains of the Shackles ply turbulent seas. Among these deadly raiders sails the vengeful Elreth "Grudge" Treeg, captain of the *Teeth of Araska* and, some believe, a villain who has somehow garnered the favor of Calistria herself. Captain Grudge and his crew range far, sailing the western coast of Avistan and Garund, preying upon the merchant vessels of many nations. In his twenty-year career he survived ambushes by the Chelish Navy, stole buried treasures hidden by his fellow Free Captains, and carried out three lifetimes of vendettas against those foolish enough to cross him. Yet not all of Captain Grudge's debts are settled.

"Teeth of Araska" is an adventure for four 4th-level characters. In addition to working as a stand-alone adventure, this Set Piece can be used to supplement this month's Adventure Path installment, "Children of the Void," or any other nautical campaign.

ADVENTURE HOOKS

GMs who choose to pit their PCs against the *Teeth of Araska* can do so in several ways. Adventure hooks marked with an asterisk might be especially useful to GMs running "Children of the Void."

Easy Pickings*: Rumors of the star strike on Devil's Elbow have spread far and fast. Anticipating the interest in such a rare event, the *Teeth of Araska* set full sail for the waters near Devil's Elbow, intent on preying upon crews too distracted by skymetal fever to consider pirates. As fate would have it, the PCs' vessel is the first Grudge and his crew encounter.

Pilfered Plunder: The PCs come into possession of a treasure map marking the location of some fabulously valuable, magical, or otherwise desired item. Upon tracking it to its source, though, they discover their loot stolen and the *Teeth of Araska* sailing away into the distance. Now the PCs must race after the pirates before the vessel can reach a friendly port and offload its booty.

Captain Venjam had us battened down for the oncoming storm, and by the time we saw them, we'd drifted into irons. I thought the pirates had to be mad to sail in such weather, but as we tried to right ourselves, I spotted the prow: three blades, like jagged teeth. And I saw the captain's face turn white.

The captain was still a first mate when the fleet ambushed the Araska near Corentyn five years past, but they say old Grudge has a long memory. The storm began to thrash us, but their ship sailed straight in, laughing at waves that nearly capsized us. I knew if we fought, he'd kill us all to get to his target. So yes, I drew my sword on my captain, and I prayed old Grudge's vengeance would be discerning.

—Bafra, first mate of the *Maleficar*, court martial testimony

Race and Rescue: Grudge recently captured Captain Mase Venjam of the Chelish Navy. In exchange for his life, Venjam offered the pirate captain the location of a long-lost treasure hidden by his father within the Eye of Abendego. Venjam's father hires the PCs and their vessel to track down and rescue his son.

Untimely Revenge*: More than five years ago, Clegg Zincher thoroughly embarrassed Elreth Treeg, hiring away most of the captain's crew to man his own seafaring venture. Informed of the fallen star business and Clegg's investment in its recovery, the *Teeth of Araska* has come to Riddleport hoping to steal the star right out from under Clegg.

THE TEETH OF ARASKA

Tattered, triangular sails whip wildly above the deck of a formidable vessel, driving it on with fearsome intent. Its three masts proudly display the scars of storms and past battles, and its fearsome draconic masthead bucks upon the waves with ravenous hunger. A ragged black flag snaps above the mainmast, bearing the image of a scarred red skull.

The *Teeth of Araska* is an Abendego tricorne, a broader variant of the caravel designed to handle the rough seas near the Eye of Abendego. Anyone who sees the ship's flag and makes a DC 20 Knowledge (local) check recognizes the ship as the *Teeth of Araska*, commanded by the vengeful Captain Elreth Treeg, also known as "Captain Grudge."

FIGHTING THE ARASKA

An encounter with the *Teeth of Araska* is likely to develop in one of two ways: deadly ship-to-ship combat involving the crews of both the PCs' ship and the pirates' vessel, or with the PCs sneaking aboard the pirate ship. A direct fight with the entire crew of the *Araska* is a deadly proposition, as all 21 crewmen, Ishana, Captain Grudge, and his pet lizards make for a CR 9 encounter—not an insurmountable battle for a 4th-level party, especially if the party recruits the help of their ship's crew, but still pretty dangerous. The adventure assumes, however, that the PCs manage to sneak aboard the ship, and it details where the *Araska*'s crew are should they be

> ### DANGER ABOARD
>
> Several sections of the *Teeth of Araska* bear noting for the special features found there.
>
> **Crow's Nest:** The crow's nest perches 60 feet above the center of area 1. It provides cover for its occupant. One can climb to the crow's nest using the rigging.
>
> **Mast:** Hardness 5, 120 hp. A destroyed mast usually brings down rigging, dealing 1d6 damage to every creature in area 1 (Reflex DC 15 negates). Creatures who fail their saves are entangled until they spend a move action to get free.
>
> **Rigging:** Hardness 0, 10 hp per 5-ft. area. Moving through the rigging requires a DC 10 Climb check.
>
> **Yard:** Hardness 5, 50 hp. Sails hang from these horizontal beams. Destroying a yard drops a sail upon area 1. Creatures here are undamaged, but are entangled until they spend a move action to get free.
>
> **Weapons and Hazards:** PCs might use ropes or hammocks as nets or turn any of a dozen tools into a makeshift club, like a belaying pin or loading hook. In areas 1, 6, 12, and 13, there is a 40% chance that an item capable of being used as an improvised weapon lies within reach.

caught unawares. Even if the PCs choose to take a subtle approach to dealing with the pirates, if the ship's alarm is raised—either by alert crewmen in area 1 or any sizable commotion below decks—their infiltration could easily turn into a sizable, multiple area battle. GMs should feel free to use "Teeth of Araska"—either as cross-ship pirate encounter or piratical dungeon-crawl—in whatever manner best suits their game.

1. Main Deck (EL 5)

Three sturdy masts rise above the marred wood of this broad deck. Although well scrubbed, fiery scars and the gashes of boarding axes mar the dark wood. Above swings a webwork of rigging and ropes, connected to the yards and crow's nest. Two longboats hang above a hatch leading below, while nearby a smaller trapdoor also stands closed. To the ship's aft, twin pairs of stairs rise up to the sterncastle, where the ship's wheel and a

Teeth of Araska

one square = 5 feet

This is Captain Treeg's sanctuary, from where he does most of his brooding and plotting. His collection of maps and charts is quite impressive, and anyone who spends a minute examining them notices they come from dozens of different sources: Chelish naval diagrams, Osirian star charts, barely legible pirate maps, and others. The entire collection is worth upwards of 120 gp. Any character who spends an hour and employs these maps to make a Knowledge (geography) or Profession (navigator) check to navigate gains a +2 circumstance bonus to his roll.

Those who investigate the floor of the room, making a DC 20 Search check, discover a hidden trap door—Captain Grudge's escape hatch—that leads to area **12** below.

Creature: Captain Grudge spends most of his time here, poring over his charts and ledgers of past slights.

CAPTAIN ELRETH "GRUDGE" TREEG   CR 5

Male human ranger 1/bard 4
NE Medium humanoid
Init +2; **Senses** Listen −1, Spot +1

DEFENSE

AC 16, touch 13, flat-footed 14
   (+3 armor, +1 deflection, +2 Dex)
hp 26 (4d6+1d8+5)
Fort +4, **Ref** +8, **Will** +3

OFFENSE

Speed 30 ft. (6 squares)
Melee +1 rapier +7 (1d6+1/18–20) or
   mwk whip +7 (1d3 nonlethal)
Special Attacks bardic music (4/day–countersong, *fascinate*,
   inspire courage +1, inspire competence), favored enemy
   (humans +2)
Spells Known (CL 4th)
   2nd (1/day)—*heroism, pyrotechnics* (DC 14)
   1st (3/day)—*animate rope, charm person* (DC 13), comprehend
     languages
   0 (3/day)—*detect magic, ghost sound* (DC 12), *know direction,*
     light, message, read magic

TACTICS

Before Combat Grudge casts *heroism* on himself at the first sign of
   danger. If the *Araska* attacks the PCs' ship, or the alarm is raised,
   Grudge attempts to rally his crew, shouting threats in a rather
   unorthodox use of inspire courage.
During Combat Grudge stalks through battle brazenly, standing
   tall and shouting orders. He looks for opportunities to
   humiliate the PCs, such as disarming. If on deck, he can cast
   animate rope on nearly any open square to create further chaos.
Morale If reduced to fewer than 10 hit points, Grudge seeks out
   Ishana for healing. If she can't be found, though, he refuses to
   let himself be taken alive, and in his pride fights to the death.

STATISTICS

Str 10, **Dex** 14, **Con** 12, **Int** 13, **Wis** 8, **Cha** 15

Base Atk +4; **Grp** +4

Feats Combat Expertise, Improved Trip, Weapon Finesse, Track

Skills Balance +6, Bluff +11, Concentration +3, Diplomacy +5, Disguise +3, Gather Information +5, Intimidate +9, Knowledge (arcana) +3, Knowledge (geography) +5, Knowledge (nature) +7, Perform (oratory) +11, Profession (sailor) +3, Sense Motive +3, Spot +1, Survival +5, Swim +3

Languages Common, Elven

SQ bardic knowledge +5, wild empathy +3

Gear +1 *rapier*, masterwork whip, masterwork studded leather, *ring of protection +1*, spyglass, keys to area **9** and the brig in area **14**

Treasure: Grudge keeps his favorite trophies here, most crafted from the bones of those who slighted him. While disturbing and intricate, they are not well maintained and are kept for their sentimental value alone. A seller would be hard pressed to get more than 20 gp for the whole lot. Among these are several ledgers tersely noting names and slights against Captain Grudge. Although worthless, anyone who spends 10 minutes flipping through the folios discovers the names Clegg Zincher and Mase Venjam among hundreds of others.

6. Middle Hold

Dim light filters through the planks above, illuminating a sizable chamber cluttered with a collection of cargos and ship's supplies. A heavy wooden grate in the floor leads below, as does a trap door near the stern. Squat, rickety doors head toward both the aft and stern.

This hold stores the majority of the ship's everyday supplies. Determined PCs who spend 20 minutes cataloging the room's inventory discover 70 gp worth of useful adventuring gear (including a hooded lantern, a few grappling hooks, several sacks, and a lot of hemp rope).

The trap door here leads to area **13**.

7. Crew Commons (EL 4)

A dozen hammocks swing between narrow beams throughout this room, swaying amid the stink of sweat and spilled rum. A splintered ladder leads up to the deck, while three doors head to the ship's aft and another, smaller door heads to the stern. Several empty bottles clink together, rolling across the floor with the ship's swaying.

Creatures: During the day, this room is usually empty except for a single working or convalescing pirate. At night, the majority of the crew rests here, spending their off time sleeping or gambling.

ARASKA PIRATES (9)

Male human warrior 1

hp 5 each (see page 66)

Treasure: Those who spend 10 minutes rifling through the room and make a DC 15 Search check turn up the scant treasures of the *Araska*'s crew amid their hammocks and scattered bundles: 6 gp, 44 sp, two half-full bottles of rum, a pair of unbalanced dice, numerous parrot feathers, a wooden holy symbol of Gozreh, three pairs of well-worn boots, two dented short swords, and a black eye patch.

8. Tralter's Quarters (EL 1/2)

The simple wooden door to this room is locked. It can be unlocked using a DC 22 Open Lock check or the key crewman Tralter keeps on his person.

The owner of this tidy bedroom left an appraiser's scale prominently displayed in a case beside the bed. A single dagger lies embedded in the floorboards, surrounded by hundreds of similar puncture holes.

This bedroom belongs to Tralter, the ship's accountant. The scales here are simple merchant's scales Tralter uses to divvy up the crew's earnings. A locked footlocker at the base of the bed (DC 25 Open Lock check to open) contains ledgers of the ship's treasure, what the captain owes to each crewman, and Tralter's own cache of 12 gp, 213 sp, and a rare treasure: an ancient, barnacle-caked silver Azlanti signet ring (worth 50 gp to a collector or historian).

Creature: Tralter likes to stay in his room so no one can steal from him.

TRALTER

Male human warrior 1

hp 5 (see page 66)

9. Rum Stores

This cramped room stores the *Teeth of Araska*'s mostly empty supply of rum and cheap wine. An obvious trap door in the ceiling leads up to area **5**.

10. Selis's Quarters (CR 2)

The room's simple wooden door is locked. It can be unlocked using a DC 22 Open Lock check or the key held by Selis.

Dozens of eerie, hand-drawn portraits decorate the walls of this sparse bedroom, and an empty birdcage hangs in one corner. Low on the starboard wall juts a strange series of levers.

This room belongs to Selis, the ship's elven wizard and lookout. A simple, lockless wooden footlocker lies beneath the bed, holding a few charcoal pencils, several pieces of sullied parchment, a whittling knife, and a small block of wood mutilated into the shape of a lopsided mermaid.

A mechanism in the starboard wall causes the doors of area 11 to slam shut while simultaneously opening a small grate near the floor between the two rooms.

Creatures: Although Selis's days are spent in the crow's nest, he spends most of his nights here, drawing, whittling, or brooding on times long past. If anyone enters area 11 while he's here, he's allowed a Listen check to notice. A round after detecting someone in the adjacent hall, he pulls the lever on the starboard wall, which slams and locks both of the hall doors. Then he uses a *scroll of summon swarm* and sends the swarm through the grate connecting

the rooms to terrorize the intruders. Selis cannot attack or be attacked through this opening, but he eagerly mocks those caught in his trap.

Captian
Elreth
"Grudge"
Treeg

SELIS   CR 2

Male elf ranger 1/sorcerer 1

CE Medium humanoid (elf)

Init +3; **Senses** low-light vision; Listen +3, Spot +7 (+10 in bright light)

DEFENSE

AC 16, touch 13, flat-footed 13

  (+3 Dex, +3 armor)

hp 10 (1d8+1d4)

Fort +3, **Ref** +5, **Will** +4 (+6 vs enchantments)

OFFENSE

 Speed 30 ft. (6 squares)

  Melee longsword +1 (1d8/19–20)

  Ranged mwk shortbow +5 (1d6/×3)

  Special Attacks favored enemy (humans +2)

  Spells Known (CL 1st, spell failure 15%)

  1st (4/day)—*shield, true strike*

  0 (5/day)—*dancing lights, detect magic, light, message*

TACTICS

During Combat At long range, Selis casts *shield* and *true strike* and fires arrows, using his wand if he misses more often than not. If enemies near, he begins using his scrolls.

Morale Selis has little loyalty, and flees to his quarters if injured. Once there, he lies in wait, hoping to use the trap he's set up.

STATISTICS

Str 10, **Dex** 17, **Con** 10, **Int** 8, **Wis** 13, **Cha** 14

Base Atk +1; **Grp** +1

SQ summon familiar (hawk), wild empathy +2

Feats Dodge, Track

Skills Climb +4, Hide +7, Knowledge (nature) +4, Listen +3, Spellcraft +0, Spot +7, Survival +5

Languages Common, Elven

Combat Gear *scroll of flaming sphere* (2), *scroll of summon swarm* (2), *scroll of web, wand of magic missile* (1st level; 27 charges); **Other Gear** masterwork studded leather, masterwork shortbow, 40 arrows, *feather token* (anchor)

11. Murder Hall

A short, narrow hall leads to a battered door bearing the sign "Food Stores."

Anyone who makes a DC 18 Search check on either of the good wooden doors here notices that it bears a lock and spring mechanism that connects with the adjacent room. A DC 20 Search check of the wall also detects the slots that connect this room with area 10.

Should the mechanism in area 10 be used to trap someone in this room, either door can be unlocked with a DC 20 Open Lock check.

12. Ship Stores

These areas are simply food stores and supply rooms. The first time a character spends 10 minutes investigating one of these store rooms and succeeds at a DC 16 Search check, he reveals 10 gp worth of useful adventuring gear and 1d6 stray gold pieces, but little else of interest.

The storerooms at the ship's aft are connected by a steep, rickety stairway.

13. Main Hold (EL 4)

Stacked crates and barrels, most of them labeled with the names of prominent merchant or military navies, turn the hold into a small maze. Captured flags hang along the walls.

Captain Treeg keeps the majority of his ship's plunder here, along with the flags of sunken or raided ships. Most of the crates are marked with words in Common, noting a variety of contents and the names of former owners—like the Aspis Consortium, West Sea Brokerage, and Sargava Shipping. Opening and cataloging all of the crates and chests in this room takes nearly two hours, though one can read the contents on most of the crates in a matter of 5 minutes to get an feel for the general contents of the hold's treasure.

If the PCs are aboard the *Teeth of Araska* searching for stolen goods, they find them here.

Creature: When not on deck with Grudge, the captain's two Lirgen dragons doze in the cool darkness here. These foul tempered animals attack anyone besides Ishana or Captain Grudge who enters the room.

FERRIS & ORBAND, LIRGEN DRAGONS   CR 2
hp 22 each (monitor lizard, MM 275)

Treasure: Ambitious PCs discover 300 gp worth of trade goods—Rahadoumi brass, Taldan lace, a variety of Osirian papyruses and incense, and fine silks from the Chitterwood of Isger. In addition, there's a shipment of 20 well-crafted longspears from Nirmathas (worth 100 gp), a well-packed crate holding 10 flasks of alchemist's fire from Alkenstar (worth 200 gp), and 400 gp of fine Ustalavic wine. Any PC who makes a DC 25 Search check also finds, wrapped in leather at the bottom of a crate of dented brass lamps, an *eversmoking bottle*.

14. Brig (EL 3)

Stout iron bars divide this room, creating a sizable cell. Evidence of past prisoners is obvious from the desperate scratches, broken bits of glass and dishware, and the unsettling stains that mar the floors and walls. A heavy iron door with a sturdy lock offers the only break in the wall of bars.

This single cell serves as the ship's brig. The iron bars and doors are rusted but sturdy. The cell can be opened using either Captain Grudge's key or by making an Open Lock check. While a DC 25 Open Lock check opens the cell door, it also springs the room's trap. A DC 30 check opens the door and bypasses the lock. Failing at either of these checks also springs the trap.

Creatures: The brig currently holds one prisoner, the captain of the Chelish naval ship *Maleficar*, Mase Venjam (LN male aristocrat 2/warrior 2). The Chelish captain claims to know the location of a fantastic treasure hidden within the shroud of the Eye of Abendago, and is using the information in barter for his life. Grudge keeps his captive here until he has time to see if the tale proves out.

Captain Venjam is a naval officer from a noble line in good standing with the Chelish military. He offers anyone who isn't obviously a member of Grudge's crew 100 gp if they'll help him escape. Grudge cut off his thumbs and has him beaten regularly to keep him complacent, leaving him at 3 hit points. Venjam knows the trick for disabling the trap in area 3.

Trap: If Captain Grudge's key is not used to open the door to the brig, when the door is opened, the room's trap is triggered.

GRUDGE TRAP   CR 3
Type mechanical
Search DC 16; **Disable Device** DC 27

EFFECTS

Trigger location; **Reset** repair
Effect atk +15 (1d12+8/x3; all Small or larger targets within the cell)

CONCLUDING THE ADVENTURE

"Teeth of Araska" concludes when the PCs have dealt with Captain Grudge and his crew and either escape the pirate vessel, destroy it, or claim it as their own. Should the party have saved Captain Venjam from the pirates' brig he proves most grateful, rewarding them for rescuing him. He increases his reward by another 50 gp for each party member if they go so far as to drop him off in a safe port. If any members of the crew of the *Araska* have survived, Venjam also sees that they face justice.

Should either Captain Grudge or Ishana somehow survive the adventure, the PCs find them both most tenacious foes. Grudge might lie in wait for years, returning to harass the PCs when next their journeys take them to the seas, or even just to a port city. Ishana proves brasher, however, seeking revenge against them with religious zeal, following them wherever they might travel. Even if these villains survive, though, dispatching the *Teeth of Araska* and scattering its crew eases the minds of countless merchants and sailors all along Avistan's coast.

Darkest Before the Fall

26 Lamashan, 4707 AR

I dug the fingers of my left hand more firmly into the gritty rock and inched my right hand up over the lip of the chasm. Rocks sliced into my knees where I pressed them against the cliff face, as if by sheer force I could stick myself to the wall. Sweat ran down my back in sticky streams, cooled instantly by the chill underground air. My eyes strained to make out shapes in the blackness—I cursed the ill fortune that allowed my lantern to slip from my now-aching fingers—as I quested for a handhold in the dark. With luck, with skill, and with strength I could get enough of a grip on something to pull myself up. If the ground or my arms didn't give way first.

In the pitch blackness before me, I heard the faintest of sounds. A brief but audible shuffle, perhaps a footstep.

"Is someone there?" I called. My own voice bounced back at me, small and thin in the yawning silence of the Darklands. No other reply came. I didn't think it possible my position could grow more precarious, but the thought of an unknown predator out there added a layer of uncertainty.

"Hello!" I called, risking the appearance of an enemy for the hope of salvation. "Is anyone there?"

As I waited, agonized, for an answer, I continued to grope for a means to pull myself up. The entire time, I reflected that on the surface roads exist where you make them, and at any time you can leave the trail and blaze your own across undiscovered country.

But underground, every passage is a potential dead end.

My journey hadn't started off badly. Once past the ancient seal and into the Darklands proper, I had found myself enchanted by the place.

I admit I'd anticipated long stretches of featureless stone tunnel, the monotony broken now and then by a stalactite, or perhaps some unusual fungi. Once I descended the flight of stone steps, obviously hewn by dwarven hammers, I found myself in a spacious, well-made tunnel stretching into blackness. Pictograms covered the walls, most depicting dwarven warriors in ornate armor battling against bizarre creatures: something like a cross between an ogre and a beetle, ambulatory mushrooms, and worms that appeared roughly the size of a two-story inn. I took my time examining the pictures as I proceeded down the tunnel—while crude, they held an arresting sort of power in their simplicity and action.

The tunnel stretched on for at least three hundred feet before it ended in a simple archway. Beyond that, a much narrower, rougher tunnel sloped sharply down. I concluded I was entering Nar-Voth, the uppermost layer of the Darklands.

Calling it a natural stone tunnel doesn't give an accurate picture. Certainly the walls were rough and the floor uneven, the stone pressed close and the air stale. The stone wasn't featureless gray, but a rippled mosaic of shades from slick black to almost bone-white, encompassing every dimension of gray and brown within, marked with veins of jade-green, rosy red, even at one point a deep sky blue. These ripples of stone ran along the wall for a few feet, or a few dozen feet, or sometimes for up to a mile. The stone didn't merely crest the wall like a wave, but occasionally broke loose and stretched to the floor or ceiling, or wove across the tunnel like a lattice, so that I was constantly climbing over or ducking under fantastic stone formations.

There was mold, often growing thick as tapestries and long as a woman's hair on the wall and floor. In one place, mold hung from ceiling to floor like a curtain, and I had to push my way though the sea-green strands, so thick it was like being underwater. Tiny leaf-green beetles, smaller than roaches, scuttled away at my passing.

The tunnel widened to cavernous proportions from time to time, and numerous smaller tunnels branched off the one I walked. I tried to choose the widest and clearest-looking turn each time I faced a choice, while still keeping with the wayfinder's heading, and did my best to record the path in my journal. I even went so far as to scratch tiny marks into the stone of the walls, though I dared not make them too obvious, lest something down here pass through and decide to investigate. Indeed, I feared something might already be doing so; whenever I paused, it seemed to me that something was watching me from just beyond my circle of lamplight, patiently waiting for me to begin moving again. I longed for dawn, then shook myself with the realization that it would never come.

The level of the tunnel rose and fell as I walked, and several times I retraced my steps to veer around an impassable gorge. I was beginning to think of campsites and how best to rest in this underground maze when the walls trembled.

I stopped dead, my hand outstretched and grazing the tunnel wall. The tremor ceased as abruptly as it had begun. Visions of cave-ins filled my head. *Not the most glorious of deaths,* I thought. *Pinned under a thousand tons of rock miles below the surface, with no one the wiser. Still, this would make one hell of a tomb.*

Regardless, I wasn't ready to lie down in my grave just yet. I inched forward cautiously, waiting to see if the tremor returned. It did, moments later, louder and even stronger. The tunnel was a wide one, almost a chamber, and the tremors seemed strongest along the wall I touched. I let go of its grimy surface and moved silently across the wide expanse to the far side.

Then the ground heaved and bucked like a living thing. I fell to one knee and my lantern skittered away in the dark. The floor opened beneath it, swallowing my little light. A keening roar echoed through the room, a screech like that of a predator but with a wet, phelgmatic quality to it. I struggled to my feet to sprint to safety, but it was too late. A chasm opened up beneath my boots and it was all I could do to catch the ledge.

The tremors faded to a low and constant tremble in the ground, and there I hung, dangling over a blackness so deep it hurt to look at, wishing for a light, a rope, a friendly face, or at the very least, that I hadn't exhausted my magical ability lighting my way.

My arms ached with the strain of bearing my weight, and it felt like red-hot pins were sliding into my shoulders. My groping right hand found a divot just deep enough to get a grip. "Cayden, or Desna," I whispered, "or anyone who might be listening, really—please let this hold my weight." I dug my fingers into the stone and heaved.

My arm held out just long enough to scrabble my boots against the stone and fling my left hand over the ledge. With both hands clutching to the rock I managed to squirm my way up onto solid ground and lie there, gasping and choking in the fine dust that now filled the cavern. In the spaces between breaths, I heard something move just beyond the reach of my vision.

"Thanks," I coughed, then lifted myself on one elbow and scanned the darkness. I could make out nothing. "Is someone there?" I tried again.

No one answered, and I heard no further footsteps. "Hmph," I muttered, wishing I had the innocence left to chalk up what I'd heard to imagination.

I fumbled in my pack for a torch and relaxed once its friendly light burst forth. I stood and made a quick circuit of this side of the chamber—now split by an eight-foot-wide gorge—but saw no trace of anyone lurking in the dark, or whatever had made that tremor and roar. I shrugged and returned to the chasm.

I could have retraced my steps and gone around, but I was convinced something lay in the darkness that way. Besides, the wayfinder still pointed in the other direction.

I lit the stubbiest of my candles and placed it at the near edge of the pit, then tossed my torch to the other side. It hit the ground, rolled and sputtered terribly, but stayed lit.

Then, out of curiosity, I tore off a bit of wrapping from a second torch and lit it, edging up to the lip of the gorge. Peering over into the blackness, I dropped the flaming fabric.

It fluttered as it fell, a winking star in the black, and for a moment I feared the distance was too great and it would flicker out in the fall. But the flame held, and after twenty or thirty feet it hit ground. I strained my eyes for anything of interest, but saw only the ridged stone.

Then I realized the flame was moving. It slid slowly to the left, and my whole body went cold as I realized the "ground" was the back of a huge, wrinkled beast. Its purplish-gray skin looked to be made of chitinous armor plating in the tiny circle of light, and I hoped desperately the beast wouldn't notice the burning on its back and look for the source. The monster filled the entire chasm—a river of hardened flesh undulating away from me—but I realized that the creature was actually a massive, wriggling worm.

I held my breath, watching its tremendous bulk writhe on and on until the candle snuffed itself out where the worm slid its bulk into a tight tunnel. Now that I was listening for it, I could hear the rasping of its body forcing its way through the rocky channel. With a queasy feeling in the pit of my stomach, I backed up, then dashed forward and hurled myself across the chasm. I skidded a little on the far side, teetered and windmilled my arms for balance, then scooped up the torch at my feet and hurried as fast as I dared away from the chamber and its disturbing occupant.

28 Lamashan, 4707 AR

By the time I'd found a place to camp, caught some restless slumber, shaken the grit out of my cloak, and followed the winding tunnels down for another few hours, I'd grown heartily sick of traveling underground.

My fatigue did not keep me from enjoying the sights, however; the territory I passed through was awe-inspiring and beautiful, in an alien sort of way. But the endless blackness, with no shred of sunlight to lift the gloom, the stale air, the constant crunch of grit beneath my boots, the ever-present chill radiating from the stone walls—all these things wore on me. It takes a special type of person to make his home underground, and I am evidently not one of them.

The tunnels grew steeper and narrower the farther I progressed, and I seemed to be walking on a down slope more often than not. I passed through a magnificent chamber with a ceiling so high it was lost in the blackness;

a stream of icy-cold water cascaded down one wall and formed a churning pool in the center of the room. I waded gingerly through the pool, staring in fascination at the oily black fish with pure white eyes that swam lazily in the water.

I also traveled through a network of tunnels that crisscrossed like a web. Phosphorescent fungus completely covered the walls; the bulbous growths lit up in unnatural shades of blue, pink, purple, and green in the light of my sunrod. (A good Pathfinder carries multiple light sources. I had three more sunrods, a couple of torches, and a handful of candles tucked into the side-pouches of my backpack, in case of emergency.) When several tunnels intersected they often formed a pocket chamber, some of which contained fungal "trees" ten or twelve feet tall. My fascination ebbed slightly when I found a malformed little skeleton half-buried in one of the trees. Its fungus-covered skull looked up at me with blank sockets, and I shivered and hurried on.

It's hard to gauge the passage of time underground, but I estimate it was around noon when I came to a side-tunnel so steeply sloped it looked more like a chimney. Sharp ridges covered the tunnel's sides, like the ripples of waves. The tunnel was narrow, but almost perfectly square, and the ridges were just the right size to form a ladder, albeit for someone slightly smaller than me. The straightness and angle of the tunnel was too perfect to be natural; someone had carved this tunnel-ladder here, which meant that something interesting probably sat at the bottom.

I leaned into the entrance and looked down as far as I could. The tunnel sloped even more sharply a few feet in, becoming a true chimney, but I saw the ridges offered numerous hand- and foot-holds.

As I peered into the black, an echo drifted up the shaft. A series of whispers in a language I didn't understand, and a moment later, an answering whisper from another voice.

Someone was down there.

At first the chimney's walls had seemed wide enough apart to allow some freedom of movement, but close enough together that I could brace my back against the wall while I descended. After a few dozen feet, though, they narrowed to the point where I had trouble stepping down—there wasn't enough room to properly bend my knee. The walls pressed in close around me and my breathing seemed loud in the narrow channel. The ridges offered secure hand-holds, but the rock abraded my skin and occasionally cut my fingers. The farther down I climbed, the narrower the chimney grew, and I began to wonder if I'd stick at some point or be forced to climb back up. So tight were the walls that I couldn't look down past my shoulders. I rested on my toes for a moment to give my arms a break, but the ridges weren't quite wide enough for me to stand on comfortably. That's when I heard the whispers again.

They came quickly, incomprehensible as before and echoing weirdly in the passage. It was as if a hundred strangers each tried to whisper a secret to me all at once. I looked around pointlessly and the whispers died.

"Hello?" I whispered. I felt a bit silly, but I'd heard enough stories of ghosts and phantasms not to discount the possibility of parlay. "Hello, is someone there?"

I remembered the sensation I'd had last time I was hanging from my fingertips and felt as if someone was watching me. Then I'd been certain there was a figure in the darkness, and no one had been there. But I knew I wasn't imagining this sound.

"Hello?" I tried again.

An explosion of light surrounded me. I cried out instinctively and shut my eyes. The whispers returned full force and a sudden breeze blew past my face. Still clinging to the wall, I cracked open my eyes.

A cloud of luminescent moths engulfed me. Each one was as large as my hand and glowed pale silver, gold, and rose. Their antennae stretched twice the length of their bodies and brushed me like a woman's hair as they swarmed around. I gasped with relief, then shuddered as the cloud continued to bat around me like drunken bumblebees. The moths seemed harmless, and I wasn't afraid of falling this time (the other day's encounter having been enough to convince me to save some of my magical reserves) but the sensation of the swarm was unsettling.

The moths remained for possibly a minute, their glow overwhelming that of my sunrod, the beat of their wings filling the passage with the susurrus I'd mistaken for whispers. Just when I was wondering if I should start to climb with the moths in tow, they continued their swarm up the chimney and vanished from sight.

"Well," I said in the silence. My sunrod seemed pale and somewhat lifeless in comparison to the moths' glow. "That was interesting. Wonder what woke them up?"

Even as I spoke the words, I remembered my hasty and somewhat irreverent prayer of the day before. Desna's symbol is the butterfly, and these silvery moths were unlike anything I'd seen before: exotic and beautiful. And I'd been hanging from my fingertips again when they'd swarmed past.

Interesting.

I continued down, wedging myself through the narrowest part of the chimney and leaving a bit of skin behind, and soon reached the tunnel to which the chimney connected. Handholds led down the wall below and I dropped the last few feet into the tunnel proper. It stood about six feet high, just enough room for me to unfold and hold my sunrod up.

This tunnel was definitely constructed, though a few side-branches seemed natural. Carvings covered the walls. They seemed similar to the ones I'd seen at the entrance to the Darklands, but so old and worn I could make out no details. I stood in the middle of the tunnel with no clear indication as to which way was "forward," so I consulted the wayfinder and marched onward.

I'd traveled for only a few hundred feet when the tunnel expanded to double its width. Another thirty, and it opened up onto a platform overlooking an ancient underground city. Domes and pillars reached like stalagmites toward the ceiling; crumbling buildings spanned the length of the cavern, close-packed palaces shunning the light from patches of glowing mold in favor of the shadows.

The first thing I did was gape. The second thing I did was sit down on the platform, so that I could gape properly while resting my legs.

The Darklands are just as dangerous for its residents.

I'm not exaggerating when I say the city was immense. In many ways it reminded me of Urgir. Though the buildings here looked considerably older, and many had actually fallen into rubble, the existing structures displayed architecture similar to Urgir's. Squat stone pillars held up heavy roofs, stone blocks as wide as my outstretched arms formed thick walls, and the streets looked grooved, bowed under the ponderous weight of marching feet. The city seemed built to withstand time and stress, and even the collapsed buildings looked solid. I got the impression they'd been knocked down, not succumbed to age.

Small figures moved among the stalactites that hung like dragon's teeth over the city; I thought they were bats, but larger than any I'd seen before. In the streets of the city I caught glimpses of movement. I tried to focus on whatever walked this ancient ruin, but the shadowy forms always slipped out of sight before I could make out details. The hairs on the back of my neck rose as the stories of ghosts and phantasms I'd recalled in the chimney came back in full force. If the dwarven dead walked anywhere, this city seemed like the perfect place.

A flash of light caught my eye. Far to my right, flames caught on a pile of something and flared up into a bonfire. The section of the city it illuminated seemed in better repair than the rest, and I saw stone blocks arranged in a crude barricade around the area. Around the fire's base I glimpsed a few stocky figures before they retreated into the darkness—dwarves, perhaps?

The scrape of a boot on stone sounded behind me. I froze, then slowly turned my head to look over my shoulder.

Two figures, both four feet tall and all muscle, stood behind me. Each one clutched a barbed spearhead mounted on a short wooden haft. Dull gray armor made their stocky forms appear even squatter, and their battered helmets glinted dully. Their eyes burned coal-red, and their skin was gray as forge smoke. I speak a little Dwarf, but I didn't have to say a word to know this pair wasn't friendly. I tried raising my empty hands and smiling, just in case.

They lunged for me, spears first, and I shouted an arcane phrase I'd been saving for just such an occasion. Flames burst from my outspread fingertips. (An empty hand doesn't always mean harmless.)

The gray dwarves bellowed and fell back a step, shielding their eyes and beating the flames out of their beards. I used the distraction to roll backward off the lip of the observation platform.

It wasn't a long drop to the ground, and I didn't use my falling spell for the simple reason that I didn't want to slow down. I got my feet under me and hit the stone hard enough to jar my teeth. The gray dwarves shouted above me and rushed to the opposite side of the platform. They began to scramble down with such agility that there must have been hidden handholds; nevertheless, my descent had been quicker than theirs. I used my head start to run. Not that I was necessarily *afraid* of the two burly, heavily armed dwarves in their native terrain, you understand. But I've been known to show remarkable common sense from time to time.

Unfortunately, running in someone else's native terrain while searching for a hiding place isn't much easier than fighting off two territorial gray dwarves—though it carries less risk of missing limbs. I barreled along as quickly as I could, searching desperately for a crevice or nook in which to conceal myself. A narrow tunnel opened up along the wall to my right and I dove in, hoping to squeeze through a passage too narrow for the armored dwarves to follow.

I found the next best thing: branching tunnels leading off in random directions. Praying with newfound piety not to hit a dead end, I veered right, then left. The tunnel narrowed and widened again, curved like a fishhook, and stopped.

I guess you can't have everything you pray for.

The end of the tunnel was a bulbous cave filled with piles of loose rubble and boulders. I turned, ready to thread my way back and try a different passage, when I heard the clatter of armor and the muttering of guttural voices. The gray dwarves had followed me, and I was afraid any movement would alert them to my presence.

I crouched behind the densest pile of rocks and stuffed the sunrod down my shirtfront, trying to breathe quietly. My lungs and legs ached from the tumble down the cliff followed by my mad dash, and I struggled not to shift and stretch too much. I strained my ears, hoping with each passing second that the sounds of pursuit would fade away.

No such luck. The clattering of armor grew louder. My heart hammered in my chest and I wiped sweat from my brow. If I had to fight, this seemed like the best place in which to make a stand, but I didn't like the odds. I'd bet gold to a Varisian that the gray dwarves could see in the dark. Making a stand might work, but I'd be happier if it didn't come to that. Besides, I had one trick left up my proverbial sleeve.

It wasn't much of a trick, to be honest—one of the first and easiest spells I ever learned. As I'd grown better at casting, the spell had grown more powerful too. At first I'd only been able to conjure the sound of a few people whispering. Now I hoped I could mimic the sounds of that ridiculously large worm I'd seen the day before.

The farther away the gray dwarves were, the better I suspected this would work. I straightened up, put my shoulder against the boulder pile, and heaved.

The topmost boulder rocked, teetered, and then crashed to the ground with an accompanying shower of gravel. I cast my spell and mimicked, as best I could from memory, the horrible keening roar of the purple worm.

As the echoes of my illusionary cry faded away, the clashing of armor stopped. I thought I heard the whisper of cautious voices ahead. I shoved the rock pile once more and another hail of stones rained down, shaking the ground as they bounced and cracked. I mimicked the worm's roar again, realistically enough to give myself shivers. I tramped around the room, shoving over rock piles and roaring like a madman. I only had a minute or so in which to make this work. Caught up in the frenzy, I could hardly listen to see if the dwarves were really backing off. Plus the chamber was full of the sound of purple worm and falling rocks.

All too quickly, the spell ended. I halted my destructive rampage, panting heavily, my arms aching and palms gritty from the effort. I cocked my head and listened.

Far in the distance, I heard the sound of armored figures quickly retreating. Silently, I celebrated.

Then the ground shook under my feet.

I spent a second frozen in shock. I wasted another breathing hard, and a third squeezing my eyes shut, before my body caught up with my brain and my legs started pumping. I bolted from the chamber at top speed, just before the ceiling caved in and the enormous bulk of the purple worm surged into the room.

I like to think my roaring dance of falling boulders was some unwitting form of purple worm poetry, and not simply a mating call or—more likely—a territorial breach that summoned the worm to see what was slithering through its home. Regardless, the worm reared its blind head, waving its torso back and forth as if scenting the air. Its maw opened, displaying slime-coated fangs that glistened in the light of the sunrod I desperately dug out of my shirt.

I risked one glance over my shoulder, then put my head down and ran like hell.

Their short legs and heavy armor hampered the gray dwarves' speed, and I passed them just as we exited into the main cavern. They lit out for the bonfire I'd seen earlier; I hightailed it in the opposite direction. The city didn't seem like a viable option—recalling those strange black shapes lurking in the shadows—so I sprinted around its perimeter until I found another tunnel in which to duck.

The sounds of keening roars, falling rocks, and, after a minute or so, dwarven screams followed me as I ran. Apparently the worm had chosen to follow the slower pair. "Excellent choice," I muttered under my breath.

Once I was certain the worm was busy feasting on the dwarves and not following me, I collapsed against the wall of the tunnel and struggled to catch my breath. I held the sunrod before me, taking comfort from its light, but even as I watched, its glow began to fade. I sat quietly, thankful for the respite—thankful to still be alive in this wondrous, dangerous place—and watched as the sunrod's light lessened bit by bit until I sat alone in darkness.

This is what happens when I try to be clever.

Bestiary

This month's entry into the *Pathfinder* Bestiary looks to the heavens! Few can say what otherworldly intelligences look down upon Golarion, regarding the unsuspecting globe with alien eyes and unspeakable intentions. This month, three of these otherworldly beings—the savage akata, ravenous moonflower, and world-walking witchwyrd—pay visits to Golarion, each extraterrestrial race eager to sate their own alien desires. Inspired by some of the most deadly beasts of sword and planet literature and science fiction cinema, these terrors eagerly intrude from unknown stars. Yet, even beyond the mysteries of space, natives of the planes and creatures of ancient legend consider Golarion as well. From the efforts of Thais, the Accidental Herald of Cayden Cailean, to the deadly desires of the sirens, fickle whims wait to seize new marks. As if the world wasn't a dangerous enough place already!

WANDERING MONSTERS

Devil's Elbow, an unremarkable spit of land near Riddleport, has undergone a most incredible change. With the crash of a star plucked from the very heavens, many eyes now turn to this simple isle. Raiders from Riddleport, eager to investigate the occurrence and perhaps recover a few chunks of rare skymetal, rush to the island, their imaginations awash with dreams of wealth and power. At the same time, though, a mysterious cabal concludes their deadly work, the drow who summoned down the calamity from above quietly gauging the effectiveness of their dreadful magic. Yet as the natives of Golarion proceed about their business, new presences, not of their world, make themselves known. And all upon a simple island, long given over to the beasts and terrible things that lair where men fear to walk.

By Calistria's Kiss, the place was alive! Alive like I've never seen. This was not the swaying wheat of fields waiting for the harvester's blade, nor the rustling canopy of a forest expectant of the axe, nor even the garden blossom grown to be plucked. Here roots recoiled from our boots, unwilling to be trod upon. Boughs bent and leaves quivered, as if spreading wordless reports of our trespass. Blooms upon vines descended from the canopy, flowering eyes seemingly curious and questioning of our intentions.

But now, my ears still ringing with Bertram's screams, the feel of his death spasm still a memory in my muscles, I feel I should have realized a most simple truth: With all life comes hunger.

—Gianco Molnar, *Intruders Upon the Heavens*

Those who dare to tread upon Devil's Elbow find the isle a brutal place, as factions from Riddleport, deadly beasts, and intruders from both above and below struggle to make the land their own.

The following descriptions detail encounters upon Devil's Elbow in greater detail.

Drow: At night, drow slink from their hidden lair to investigate their work and the intrusion of surface dwellers upon their isle. In most cases, the drow avoid encounters with surface dwellers, seeking to keep their operations on the isle secret, but if pursued, they engage in combat to deadly effect. A small band of 1d4 drow has an average EL of 6 and uses the drow guardian stats found on page 37. Drow encountered in this manner do not count against the total number of guards in the sea caves of Devil's Elbow. There are no more than eight additional drow wandering the island in this manner.

Riddleport Faction: Numerous groups from Riddleport have plans upon Devil's Elbow. Whether they be Zincher's men, Riddleport thieves and thugs (see *Pathfinder* #13), pirates, Cyphermages, or others, few of these groups have any intention of sharing their claim on the island with strangers. GMs who choose or randomly roll an encounter with Riddleport natives might create their own encounters or draw upon any of the following suggestions.

Cyphermages: The Order of Cyphers is particularly interested in the happenings upon Devil's Elbow. Although readier to talk and bargain than many of Riddleport's more nefarious groups, cyphermages can prove helpful short-term allies or deadly opponents. GMs who wish to add an encounter with Cyphermages should use the stats on page 25. This encounter can be with 1d6 additional Cyphermages who were cut off from their allies in Witchlight, and they might ask the PCs to escort them back there to safety.

Pirates: Rumors of the star that crashed near Riddleport have spread far and fast. Scavengers from across the seas have quickly descended upon Devil's Elbow, hoping to turn a quick profit or prey upon those there to turn a quick profit. Whether sailing the seas around the isle or raiding the camps of other explorers, these opportunistic scoundrels are a daring but cowardly lot. GMs who wish

DEVIL'S ELBOW RANDOM ENCOUNTERS			
d%	Creature	Avg. EL	Source
1–5	1 giant gecko	1	*Pathfinder* #1
6–9	1 axebeak	2	*Tome of Horrors*
10–13	1 hippogriff	2	MM 152
14–18	1d4 reefclaws*	2	*Pathfinder* #7
19–24	1d8 stirges	2	MM 236
25–28	1 assassin vine	3	MM 20
29–33	1d4 boars	4	MM 270
34–36	1 centipede swarm	4	See description
37–39	1 manticore	4	MM 179
40–46	2d6 wild dogs**	4	MM 272
47–52	2d4 Medium centipedes	5	MM 286
53–54	1 nightbelly boa**	5	MM 280
55–63	1d8 void zombies	5	See page 22
64	1 wraith***	5	MM 257
65–74	2d6 akatas	6	*Pathfinder* #14
75–78	1d4 harpies	6	MM 150
79–84	1d4 scrags*	7	MM 248
85–87	1 water naga*	7	MM 193
88	1 nine-headed hydra*	8	MM 155
89–97	Riddleport faction	—	See description
98–99	Drow***	—	See description
100	1 dragon turtle*	9	MM 88
* If near the seashore, otherwise reroll this result			
** Local animals (giant constrictor snake or riding dog)			
*** Night only, reroll if this result arises during the day			

to run a pirate encounter should see this volume's Set Piece adventure, "Teeth of Araska." An encounter with 2d6 Araska pirates (see page 66) has an average EL of 4.

Riddleport Toughs: Many of the groups exploring Devil's Elbow are not friendly. Whether they be simple thugs hoping to find a few pieces of skymetal or mercenaries hired to reclaim the entire fallen star, such explorers are quick to attack those edging in on their claim. A typical encounter with a group of such Riddleport toughs should use the stats for Zincher thugs on page 31 and include 2d8 opponents, making for a EL 5 encounter on average.

During Combat Akatas work together, following the cues of the largest member of their pack and driving foes toward either treacherous footing or strong pack members. Those acting on their own attempt to set up ambushes for their opponents, preferring to pounce from above. Akatas work together to surround their foes and flank enemies whenever possible.

Morale An akata fights to the death as long as at least one other akata within sight is also fighting.

STATISTICS

Str 12, **Dex** 15, **Con** 12, **Int** 3, **Wis** 12, **Cha** 11

Base Atk +1; **Grp** +2

Feats Improved Initiative

Skills Balance +4, Climb +9, Move Silently +6, Tumble +7

SQ hibernation

ECOLOGY

Environment any

Organization solitary, pair, or pack (3–30)

Treasure none (but see text below)

Advancement 3–8 HD (Medium); 9–14 HD (Large); 15–20 HD (Huge)

Level Adjustment —

SPECIAL ABILITIES

Deaf (Ex) Akatas cannot hear. They are immune to spells and effects that rely on the target's hearing to function, but they cannot make Listen checks.

Hibernation (Ex) Akatas can enter a state of hibernation for an effectively infinite number of years. Akatas do not take damage from starvation. Should an akata go for 3 or more days without eating, it seeks out a place to hibernate and then surrounds itself with a layer of fibers that quickly hardens into a cocoon made of skymetal known as noqal. An akata remains in a state of hibernation until it senses another living creature within 10 feet or after it is exposed to extreme heat. An akata awakened from its noqal cocoon can claw its way out in 1d4 minutes.

No Breath (Ex) Akatas do not breathe, and as such are immune to inhaled toxins (but not odor-based effects).

Salt Water Vulnerability (Ex) Due to their bizarre physiology, salt water acts as an extremely strong acid to akatas. Even a splash of salt water deals 1d6 points of damage to an akata, and full immersion in salt water deals 4d6 points of damage per round. An akata corpse submerged in salt water completely dissolves in 1 minute.

Void Bite (Ex) Akatas hold hundreds of microscopic larval young within their mouths, spreading these parasitic larvae to hosts through their bite. Once spread to a creature, the larvae leech off a humanoid host. Only humanoids make suitable hosts for akata young—all other creature types are immune to this parasitic infection. The infection itself is known as void death, and it can be cured in the same methods as normal diseases. Creatures that are immune to disease are also immune to an akata's void bite.

AKATA

This bizarre creature has the shape of a lion, but its hairless body shimmers a shade of oily blue. Where a noble mane should be instead quiver and twitch dozens of thick tentacles, probing and lashing out at the air around a fierce, many-fanged maw. Behind the beast, connected to the hindquarters of a predatory body of strange musculature and proportions, whips a pair of long tentacular tails. The creature itself is swift and sure in its movements, yet is also unnervingly silent.

AKATA   **CR 1**

Always N Medium aberration

Init +6; **Senses** darkvision 120 ft., scent; Listen —, Spot +1

DEFENSE

AC 13, touch 12, flat-footed 11

   (+2 Dex, +1 natural)

hp 11 (2d8+2)

Fort +1, **Ref** +2, **Will** +4

Defensive Abilities deaf, no breath; **Immune** cold, disease, fire, poison, suffocation; **SR** 15

Weakness saltwater vulnerability

OFFENSE

Spd 40 ft.; climb 20 ft.

Melee bite +2 (1d6+1 plus void death) and

   2 tendrils –3 (1d3)

Void Death—bite, Fortitude DC 12, incubation period 1 hour, damage 1d3 Dex and 1d3 Con. Should a creature perish while infected, it rises as a void zombie 2d4 hours later (see below).

Skills An akata has a +8 racial bonus on Climb checks and can always choose to take 10 on Climb checks, even if rushed or threatened. In addition, akatas are unnaturally quiet, and have a +4 racial bonus on Move Silently checks.

Terrifying predators that dwell in the vast blackness of space, akatas make their homes on dying planets, asteroids, meteors, and even comets. Many believe that the akatas somehow survived the violent destruction of their home world by clinging to the chunks of stone left behind after the planet's catastrophic death.

A typical akata stands 3 1/2 feet tall. Being particularly dense for their size, these creature's rubbery bodies often weigh upwards of 400 pounds.

ECOLOGY

As akatas cannot hear and they lack anything resembling lungs and vocal chords with which to make sounds, akatas communicate via visual and olfactory means. For long-range communication outside of line of sight, the akatas use special scent glands on their necks just behind their jawbones to produce a bewildering (and sometimes stomach-turning) array of different smells that they spray out in fine mists. The creatures have no need to breathe, and can "taste" scents with their tongues. When two akatas can see one another, they use tail motion and eye color to communicate—akatas can force their eyes to change color to a thousand different shades. No known method of discerning the meanings of these elaborate and nuanced color codes has ever been developed.

Although akatas do not carry treasure, an akata cocoon is made of a combination of hardened resin from the creature's pores and a rare metal called noqual. An akata cocoon contains 10 pounds of noqual, worth a total of 500 gp, but in order to harvest the material one needs to find an unhatched cocoon, since akatas typically eat the remnants of their cocoons when they emerge.

HABITAT & SOCIETY

Akatas live in the depths of outer space. Most hibernate in small colonies, sleeping for countless years on the surfaces of small meteors and asteroids, waiting patiently for the time when their rocky homes might crash onto a planet or other object that can support life. When surrounded by animal life of any kind, the akatas become relentless attackers, often driving entire planets (or at least salt-water-surrounded continents) extinct.

Akatas live in social groups comprised of no more than 30 individuals, with the largest of these groups led by massive members of their race known as akata princes.

VOID ZOMBIES

Many humanoids that face akatas become carriers of their attackers' next generation. Infested with larval akatas, such victims suffer the ravages of void death. Although particularly hearty and tenacious individuals might last for weeks, void death is often fatal.

But the victim's death marks only the beginning of this alien terror.

Those who perish while suffering from void death become void zombies. Within 2d4 hours of a carrier's death, the strongest of the akata larvae infesting the corpse worms its way to the humanoid's brain and undergoes a swift gestation. This accelerated growth causes the feeler-covered head of the oversized, tadpole-like parasite to latch onto the base of its victim's brain and reenergize the dying organ, taking total control. These parasite-possessed corpses are known as void zombies. As akata larvae are too large to fit wholly within the skulls of most of Golarion's humanoid races, these zombies have a distinctive appearance, with the fanged tail of the parasite bursting through its host's jaw, dangling forth from the broken skull.

A void zombie has the same statistics as a humanoid zombie with the following additional abilities. The stats for a typical void zombie appear on page 22.

Speed: Unlike a normal zombie, a void zombie can run. In addition, a void zombie does not possess the zombie's single action only special quality.

Attacks: In addition to its normal slam attack, a void zombie gains a secondary "tongue" attack (actually the larval akata's feeding tendril that hangs from the zombie's ruined jaws) that deals 1d6 points of damage.

Blood Drain (Ex): If a void zombie hits a living creature with its tongue attack, it drains blood from the creature, inflicting 2 points of Strength damage before the tongue detaches.

Vulnerable to Critical Hits: While a void zombie retains a standard zombie's damage reduction of 5/slashing, they do not enjoy the typical undead immunity to critical hits and sneak attacks. A critical hit or sneak attack made against a void zombie indicates damage to the larval akata growing within its body.

CR: When determining a void zombie's CR, treat it as if it were one category higher than normal—a 2 HD void zombie is thus CR 1, not 1/2.

Lifespan: Akata larvae require 1d4 weeks to gestate. After that time, they are ready to make the transformation into adult akatas. Void zombies bearing akata larvae ready to emerge seek out a secluded area and "vomit" their child into a shallow hole or crevice. The void zombie then "dies," toppling over the disgorged larva. A scant 2d6 hours later, a full-grown akata emerges, usually taking the rotting corpse as its first meal.

Defensive Abilities plant traits; **DR** 10/slashing; **Immune** electricity; **Resist** cold 10

Weakness vulnerability to fire

OFFENSE

Spd 20 ft.

Melee bite +16 (2d6+9) and 2 tentacles +11 (1d8+4)

Space 15 ft.; **Reach** 15 ft.

Special Attacks improved grab, light pulse, pod prison

TACTICS

During Combat A moonflower attacks those closest to it, trying to use its improved grab ability on any creature within reach. If threatened by multiple opponents, it uses its light pulse to disorient enemies and attempts to use its pod prison while its victim's allies can't be of aid.

Morale Solitary moonflowers flee if reduced to less than a third of their hit point total. In groups, moonflowers fight to the death, fleeing only when a sole plant survives.

STATISTICS

Str 28, **Dex** 10, **Con** 25, **Int** 5, **Wis** 12, **Cha** 17

Base Atk +9; **Grp** +26

Feats Blind-Fight, Improved Initiative, Improved Sunder, Power Attack, Stealthy

Skills Hide –6 (+10 in thick vegetation), Listen +4, Move Silently +8, Spot +5

Languages telepathy (1 mile, other moonflowers only)

SQ pod spawn

ECOLOGY

Environment any

Organization solitary or cluster (2–10)

Treasure standard

Advancement 13–18 HD (Huge); 19–28 HD (Gargantuan); 29–34 HD (Colossal)

Level Adjustment —

SPECIAL ABILITIES

Improved Grab (Ex) To use this ability, a moonflower must hit a creature at least one size smaller than itself with its bite attack. It can then attempt to start a grapple as a free action without provoking an attack of opportunity. If it wins the grapple check, it establishes a hold and can use its pod prison ability the following round.

Light Pulse (Su) As a standard action, a moonflower can release a pulse of bright light from its numerous blossoms every 1d6 rounds up to 3 times a day. All sighted creatures within 50 feet (save other moonflowers) with line of sight to the moonflower must make a DC 23 Fortitude save or be blinded for 1d4 rounds. This save is Constitution-based.

Pod Prison (Ex) Once every 1d4 rounds, a moonflower can try to swallow a grabbed opponent of a smaller size than itself by making a successful grapple check. A swallowed creature is swiftly cocooned in a tight, fibrous mass and forced out of the moonflower's space into an adjacent square of the plant's choice. Once expelled, the creature remains cocooned and

MOONFLOWER

Long, velvety green tendrils extend from a massive green trunk. A knot of roots stands exposed, branching out from the base, raising the immense plant off the ground. Giant clusters of blossoms and pulsing nodules sprout from the plant, occasionally shedding a dim, repulsive glow. It's enough, almost, to distract from the writhing tendrils and the giant, oddly toothed clamshell leaves that betray a life no plant should have.

MOONFLOWER   **CR 8**

N Huge plant

Init +4; **Senses** darkvision 60 ft., low-light vision; Listen +4, Spot +5

DEFENSE

AC 20, touch 8, flat-footed 20 (+12 natural, –2 size)

hp 138 (12d8+84); fast healing 5

Fort +15, **Ref** +4, **Will** +5

takes 2d8+8 points of bludgeoning damage and 8 points of acid damage per round from the living cocoon's pulsing, acid-filled innards. A cocooned creature can cut its way out by using a light slashing or piercing weapon to deal 25 points of damage to the cocoon's insides (AC 15). Others can aid a cocooned creature by attacking with slashing or piercing weapons, but in addition to the damage dealt to the cocoon, the creature inside takes half the damage of an attack. Once the creature exits, the cocoon deflates and is destroyed. Other swallowed opponents are cocooned in their own pods.

Pod Spawn (Ex) Should a moonflower's pod prison be allowed to kill and digest a Small or larger creature, 1d4 hours later it transforms into an adult moonflower with full hit points. The newly formed moonflower has its own consciousness, but some aspect of its trunk or blossoms resembles the creature that died within. The dead creature's equipment remains inside the new moonflower and can only be retrieved by killing the alien plant.

Skills A moonflower gains a +16 racial bonus on Hide checks made in thick vegetation.

A fully-grown moonflower stands easily 20 feet tall with a massive trunk that is frequently 4 feet or more in diameter. The roots extend away from the base and into the soil, making the plant seem well anchored, but the roots themselves possess an agility that belies the great size of the plant and allows the moonflower to uproot itself and move with surprising speed. The tendrils of the plant are independently prehensile and writhe around the large flytrap-like "head" that crowns the stem. Bulbous growths and budding protuberances pulse and quiver along the alien plant's trunk and thrum with cosmic light.

Moonflowers have never been known to communicate with the natives of Golarion, even druids and others who regularly converse with plants. The plants do possess some manner of strange telepathy, though, being in constant communication with their nearby brethren at all times. Those who manage to intrude upon the creatures' alien thoughts face an assault of horrible visions of terrifying worlds covered by jungles ancient, sentient, and malign.

ECOLOGY

First discovered in Numeria generations ago, these alien plants endanger the entirety of Golarion. Undeterred by hostile environments, moonflowers thrive wherever they can find food. Unfortunately for the races of Golarion, the moonflower prefers fresh meat. The life of a moonflower is exceedingly short, and few live longer than a month. They develop quickly, reaching full size in mere hours. Some rare specimens grow to incredible proportions, rivaling the heights of castle turrets, but all known examples of such creatures have been exterminated.

PLANTS FROM SPACE!

"All plants move. They don't usually pull themselves out of the ground and chase you! If we could find out how this thing functions we might figure out an easier way of killing it."

—John Wyndham, *Day of the Triffids*

Alien plants have long found their way into entertainment: from the triffids of John Wyndham's *Day of the Triffids;* to the alien pod people of Jack Finney's novel *The Body Snatchers* and its superlative big-screen spawn, 1956's and 1978's *Invasion of the Body Snatchers* and 1993's *Body Snatchers;* to the infamous "Feed Me!" of Seymore's Audrey II in Charles B. Griffith's *Little Shop of Horrors*. Roleplaying games are also no stranger to hungry plants from space, like those that appeared in 1980's *Expedition to the Barrier Peaks*. The moonflower owes its inspiration to these predecessors and dozens of other muses not of this world.

Moonflowers possess simple intelligences, but they are also driven by overriding impulses. They know all too well that once their cosmic journey drops them on soil, their race has an unbearably finite span in which to spread and feed. One in a hundred moonflowers possesses the potential to grow to massive size and bud the organs necessary to jettison a cloud of seedpods into space, furthering the foul plants' spread through the cosmos. Only by consuming and converting as many creatures as possible can the moonflowers hope to continue their scourge of the worlds.

Moonflowers rarely move about during the day except to protect themselves. Like most plant creatures, they do not sleep, and they take all worthwhile opportunities to feed upon careless creatures that approach in daylight.

HABITAT & SOCIETY

Alien and unknowable, the moonflowers cluster themselves together as their numbers grow, the largest of them herding the others toward whatever life they can find and consume. Hardy beyond reason, these plants can travel and live freely in almost any environment. Moonflowers breathe through their root systems and can be impeded by water barriers.

Despite their lack of natural predators on Golarion, moonflower herds are rare. Most intelligent creatures recognize the plants' alien nature and are unsettled by the unexpected appearance of large clusters—especially those that could not have possibly grown over night. Once a herd has formed, however, it becomes a force as dangerous as any major natural disaster. In rare cases, a moonflower that has achieved Gargantuan size or greater will start a cyclical colony, spreading terror for 6 months or more and then going dormant for years or even decades before starting the cycle again.

Before Combat A siren uses her inspire courage bardic music ability before entering combat, bolstering herself, her charmed humanoid companions (if any), and any other non-siren allies, but never other sirens.

During Combat A siren always opens combat with her siren song, judging which effect of the versatile ability best suits the situation and her mood at the moment. A siren always leaves alive the character with the highest Charisma score under the effect of her captivating song, allowing her to later attempt to gain control over that creature with *charm person.*

Morale While a siren's charmed allies might gladly fight to the death to protect her, the feeling is not mutual. A siren happily sacrifices her charmed protectors in order to save her own life. If her humanoid companion goes down or she is reduced to 20 hit points or fewer, she flees and seeks a high, isolated place to rest and recover.

STATISTICS

Str 10, **Dex** 19, **Con** 12, **Int** 14, **Wis** 19, **Cha** 21

Base Atk +8; **Grp** +8

Feats Dodge, Flyby Attack, Lightning Reflexes

Skills Hide +9, Knowledge (history) +8, Listen +15, Perform (sing) +16, Spot +15

Languages Auran, Common

ECOLOGY

Environment temperate or warm hills

Organization solitary or flight (2–7)

Treasure standard

Advancement by character class; **Favored Class** bard

Level Adjustment +4

SPECIAL ABILITIES

Bardic Music (Su) A siren may use bardic music as a bard of a level equal to half her racial Hit Dice. If she gains actual levels in bard, these levels stack for the purpose of determining what bardic music effects she has access to.

A typical siren uses Perform (sing) and can use the following bardic music abilities: countersong, *fascinate,* inspire competence, and inspire courage. A siren may use her siren song without interrupting a use of her bardic music ability.

Siren Song (Su) The siren's most infamous weapons are her songs. When a siren sings, all creatures (other than sirens) within a 300-foot spread must succeed on a DC 19 Will save or become enthralled (see below). The effect depends on the type of song the siren chooses and continues for as long as the siren sings and for 1 round thereafter. All the effects of a siren's songs are sonic mind-affecting effects. A creature that successfully saves cannot be affected again by any of that siren's songs for 1 hour. The save DC is Charisma-based. A bard's countersong ability allows the captivated creature to attempt a new Will save.

Enthralled creatures behave in one of the following four ways, as the siren chooses when she begins singing.

SIREN

This strange creature looks like a bird with meticulously preened plumage. Rather than an avian head, though, its face is that of a beautiful human woman with locks of long, shining hair. Despite her comely features, her talons look no less deadly than those of some gigantic hawk.

SIREN   **CR 5**

Usually CN Medium magical beast

Init +4; **Senses** darkvision 60 ft., low-light vision; Listen +15, Spot +15

DEFENSE

AC 18, touch 14, flat-footed 14

  (+4 Dex, +4 natural)

hp 44 (8d8+8)

Fort +7, **Ref** +12, **Will** +6

Immune mind-affecting effects

OFFENSE

Spd 30 ft.; fly 60 ft. (good)

Melee 2 talons +8 (1d4)

Special Attacks bardic music, siren song

Spell-like Abilities (CL 7th)

  3/day—*cause fear* (DC 16), *charm person* (DC 16), *deep slumber* (DC 18), *shout* (DC 19)

TACTICS

Captivation: A captivated victim walks toward the siren, taking the most direct route available. If the path leads into a dangerous area (through flame, off a cliff, or the like), that creature gets a second saving throw. Captivated creatures can take no actions other than to defend themselves. (Thus, a fighter cannot run away or attack but takes no defensive penalties.) A victim within 5 feet of the siren stands there and offers no resistance to her attacks, should she choose to attack him. This is a charm effect.

Fascination: A transfixed victim is fascinated by the siren for as long as she continues singing. As soon as her song stops, the fascination continues for 1 additional round and then ends.

Obsession: An obsessed victim becomes defensive of the siren and does all he can to prevent harm from coming to her, going so far as attacking allies in her defense. The victim is not controlled by the siren, but views her as a cherished ally. This is a charm effect.

Slumber: A victim immediately falls asleep, rendering the creature helpless. While the siren is singing, no noise will wake the exhausted creature, though slapping or wounding him does. The creature continues sleeping for 1d4 minutes after a siren stops singing, but can be awakened by loud noises or any other normal method.

These bizarre beings have the bodies of unusually large birds—usually massive rooks, owls, or eagles—but the heads of beautiful human women. Their faces usually reflect the human ethnicity dominant in the area in which they lair, and they almost always bear a vibrant and youthful countenance.

A typical siren stands 4 1/2 feet tall, has a wing span of 8 feet, and weighs approximately 120 pounds.

ECOLOGY

The similarities in general appearance and abilities between sirens and harpies cause rousing debates regarding their origin and relations among those few who study the creatures. Many theorize that sirens might be the progenitors of the harpy race, as legends of sirens often predate those of harpies in numerous lands. Regardless of the two similar races' connections, the capricious sirens seem less motivated by maliciousness than their harpy cousins, and they are just as likely to use their songs out of curiosity or whimsy as out of hunger or defense.

As a curious and unfortunate quirk of their unknown origins, all sirens are female and—short of death from misadventure or prolonged solitude—long-lived. The oldest known sirens haunt their territories for nearly a millennium, although most only live a few hundred years. Sirens require male humanoids to mate, and several times a decade either capture or rescue bold or comely sailors who enter their territories. They also seem to take particular pride in their songs, and stories abound of sirens dying—either through heartache or suicide—when sailors they attempted to lure overcame their compelling powers and escaped their grasps.

HABITAT & SOCIETY

Sirens always live near the sea, where their powerful voices can carry over the waves and attract the attention of unwary sailors who trespass near their isles. The calls of sirens signal death, and their very name in many languages equates to "death" or "loss."

Sirens do not form a cohesive society, though occasionally a small group of such creatures might form. They completely lack sympathy for one another, and, even in these uncommon instances, they viciously compete with each other rather than cooperate.

KNOWN SIRENS

Relatively rare and always dangerous, sirens in a region tend to become local legends. A few rise to such fearsome prominence that their fame spreads across the world.

Lady Wyo: Just off the coast of Qadira, about 2 miles south of Sedeq, rises a small chunk of rock covered in verdant life and elaborate structures. This tiny island, known as Wyo's Rest, is a small paradise of gardens and greenhouses where handsome young Qadiran men go to spend several years in indentured luxury. In an agreement stretching back nearly 3 centuries, Sedeq supplies Lady Wyo with her choice of companions, who serve for 4 years or until she grows bored with them—whichever comes first. In exchange, Lady Wyo not only allows ships free passage within her territory, but she also actively comes to the aid of troubled Qadiran ships within her waters.

Thelxinoe: A menace to those sailing south of Jalmeray, the ancient siren Thelxinoe controls ocean access to a Nexian community on the small island of Karalta. Despite their best efforts, the Nexian arclords on the island have yet to dislodge her, and two even became her thralls for a short time. Such is Thelxinoe's power that those who sail the Obari speak of Thelxinoe's Toll—the need to carry beeswax with which to plug their ears in hopes of avoiding Thelxinoe's seductive song.

Virashi: The scourge of Riddleport's shipping lanes for several hundred years, Virashi finally went to her grave a few decades ago. Only once during her long tenure on Devil's Elbow (a small island south of the city but directly on its shipping lanes) did Virashi slacken in her violent outbursts and attempts to lure in sailors, a change in behavior that ultimately ended in her death. To this day, the people of Riddleport still mostly avoid Devil's Elbow, fearing that her ghost haunts the island, sending ships and their foolish crews to their graves.

Fort +18, **Ref** +21, **Will** +15; charmed life

Defensive Abilities improved evasion, uncanny dodge; **DR** 15/
lawful; **Immune** electricity, fear, petrification; **Resist** cold 10,
fire 10; **SR** 27

OFFENSE

Spd 50 ft., fly 80 ft. (good)

Melee *Tyranny's Foil* +25/+20/+15/+10 (2d8+12, 19–20/x3)

Space 10 ft.; **Reach** 10 ft.

Spell-Like Abilities (CL 15th)

At will—*freedom of movement, good hope, greater heroism, true strike*

3/day—*break enchantment, displacement, greater dispel magic,
plane shift* (self and willing targets only), *remove curse, shout*
(DC 21)

1/day—*hallow* (DC 22), *planar ally* (bralani or ghaele only), *word
of chaos* (DC 24)

TACTICS

During Combat Thais dislikes personally engaging in physical
combat, instead preferring to inspire and bolster her allies with
her aura of bravery, fortune's kisses, and the use of *good hope*
and *greater heroism*, coupled with her piercing gaze. If hard-
pressed, she grows to Huge size and makes flyby or spring
attacks with *Tyranny's Foil*.

Morale Thais withdraws from combat via *plane shift* if reduced to
40 hit points or less.

STATISTICS

Str 24, **Dex** 26, **Con** 24, **Int** 21, **Wis** 18, **Cha** 24

Base Atk +17; **Grp** +28

Feats Dodge, Flyby Attack, Hover, Improved Initiative, Lightning
Reflexes, Mobility

Skills Bluff +27, Concentration +17, Diplomacy +31, Disguise
+17, Escape Artist +18, Heal +14, Hide +14, Intimidate +9,
Knowledge (local) +15, Knowledge (religion) +15, Knowledge
(the planes) +15, Listen +24, Move Silently +28, Perform (dance)
+27, Profession (courtesan) +14, Sense Motive +24, Sleight of
Hand +20, Spot +24, Tumble +28

Languages Auran, Celestial, Common, Draconic, Infernal; *tongues*

SQ armor of valor, change shape, charmed life, fortune's kiss

ECOLOGY

Environment any

Organization solitary

Treasure none

Advancement 18–26 HD (Huge), 27–35 HD (Gargantuan)

Level Adjustment —

SPECIAL ABILITIES

Armor of Valor (Su) A halo of righteous energy surrounds
Thais, granting her a deflection bonus to her AC equal to her
Charisma bonus.

Aura of Bravery (Su) Thais is surrounded by an aura of courage
that inspires her allies. Friendly creatures in a 20-foot radius
are affected by the spells *remove fear* and *remove paralysis*.
Each ally also gains a +1 morale bonus on attack rolls, weapon
damage rolls, saves, and skill checks, while each hostile
creature takes a −1 morale penalty on such rolls.

THAIS

*A beautiful woman of regal bearing relaxes here, cutting an
imposing figure more than twice as tall as a man. Five feathered
wings, three black and two white, sprout from her back, while a
sixth appears to be missing. Blue ribbons weave across the angelic
figure's form, offering only the barest hint of modesty. She holds
a large crystalline halberd that seems to crackle and pulse with
chaotic energy.*

THAIS   **CR 15**

CG Large outsider (chaotic, extraplanar, good)

Init +12; **Senses** darkvision 60 ft., low-light vision; Listen +22,
Spot +22

Aura aura of bravery (20 ft.), piercing gaze (30 ft.)

DEFENSE

AC 33, touch 24, flat-footed 25
(+7 deflection, +8 Dex, +9 natural, −1 size)

hp 195 (17d8+119)

Change Shape (Su) Thais can assume the form of a female elf, half-elf, or human from Medium to Huge size at will.

Charmed Life (Ex) As the personification of luck, Thais gains a +1 luck bonus on all saving throws. Additionally, up to three times per day, she can choose to reroll any die roll that she makes before it results in success or failure. She must take the result of the reroll, even if it's worse than the original roll.

Fortune's Kiss (Su) Three times per day, as a standard action, Thais can blow a kiss that grants good luck to any one creature within 30 feet. The target can roll his next d20 roll twice and take the better result.

Piercing Gaze (Su) Thais's penetrating gaze burns deep into the hearts and souls of enemies within 30 feet. Lawful enemies must make a DC 25 Will save or take 5d6 points of damage and become dazed. A successful save reduces this damage by half and negates the daze effect. Non-lawful creatures are unaffected by Thais's gaze. The save DC is Charisma-based.

Tongues (Sp) Thais can speak with any creature that has a language, as if using a *tongues* spell. This ability is always active.

Tyranny's Foil *Tyranny's Foil*, also known as the Staff of Liberty, is a Large +2 *anarchic keen* halberd. In addition, three times per day, as a standard action, Thais can use the halberd to open all non-magical locked doors and bindings and break all non-magical chains and shackles within 30 feet (regardless of hardness). If *Tyranny's Foil* is ever removed from Thais' hands, she can summon the weapon back to her grasp as a free action.

The herald of Cayden Cailean is Thais, the living personification of freedom, luck, and courage, and the personal emissary of the god of bravery, freedom, and wine. She is usually sent to aid or protect Cayden Cailean's faithful, but might appear any place where slaves struggle against oppression, valiant rebels fight for freedom, the desperate and afraid need hope and courage, or when a hero needs just a little luck to further some great cause.

Thais typically appears as a beautiful, 15-foot-tall, angelic woman, but she can change her size at will to anywhere from 4 feet to 32 feet tall. She wears scandalous angelic garb, little more than blue ribbons symbolizing freedom. Thais is always depicted bearing her signature weapon, an ancient halberd borrowed from the goddess Milani's armory called *Tyranny's Foil*. Thais's wings are said to represent the Six Sacred Freedoms: Liberty, or freedom from restraint; Individuality, or freedom from coercion; Conscience, or freedom from corruption; Love, or freedom from loneliness; and Security, or freedom from fear. Her sixth wing, representing Autonomy, or freedom from oppression, is missing.

ECOLOGY

Much as Cayden Cailean himself is the "Accidental God," so could Thais be called the "Accidental Herald." Centuries ago, Thais was a hetaera, a high-class prostitute in the Gilded City of Oppara, the capital of Taldor. Before his ascension to godhood, the mortal Cayden Cailean came to know and befriend her, and the two shared a flirtatious (though never sexual) relationship. In fact, they had several adventures together, and Thais helped the young Cayden out of several difficult situations. The most famous of these is recounted in the "Tale of the Prefect's Wife," when Thais helped Cayden escape the cuckolded husband of one of his paramours by dressing him up as a courtesan like herself. Together, Thais and the disguised Cayden spent an evening entertaining the prefect and other government officials. The evening ended with another narrow escape for Cayden, this time from the amorous advances of the wine-soused prefect himself.

When Thais died years later, Cayden, already an ascended god, claimed her soul and somewhat impulsively made her his herald. Though unexpected, Thais accepted her new role with aplomb. Always one to hold her own with Cayden, Thais saw no reason to act any differently than she always had with the deity. Although their relationship is as flirty as ever, Thais remains an outspoken critic of the god and his brash (and frequently drunken) ideas. She follows his orders faithfully, but often with her own personal interpretation.

HABITAT & SOCIETY

When not at Cayden Cailean's side, Thais spends time on the Material Plane, often in the guise of her former human form. She frequently takes mortal lovers of both sexes, and over the years has even focused her attentions on the gods themselves, with rumored relationships with Aroden, Calistria, and Nethys, as well as scores of lesser deities. She is a sworn enemy of Asmodeus, however, as his portfolios of tyranny and slavery are in direct opposition to her embodied philosophy. She devotes much of her time to combating his minions, and once even foolishly faced the Prince of Darkness himself. Tricked into coming to the Nine Hells, she suffered a humiliating defeat at his hands, narrowly escaping only by sacrificing one of her wings. That wing, representing freedom from oppression, remains within Asmodeus' hellish trophy room, leaving Thais with only five wings.

Throughout Golarion, freed slaves, revolutionaries, and drunken heroes revere Thais as their patron saint. She is often depicted in Cayden Cailean's temples, warriors' halls, and in revolutionary art. Though her veneration remains traditional in Taldor and Absalom, other nations have made her their own. To the escaped slaves of the River Kingdoms, she is known as the Unfettered Lady, while the pirate lords of the Shackles honor her as Our Lady of the Fair Seas. In Andoran, she is called Andora, the national personification of the People's Revolt, and frequently figures upon the bows of the ships of the Gray Corsairs. In Galt, she was immortalized in Darl Jubannich's poetry as Cerulean Liberty, with blue wings symbolizing skies made clear by the sacrifices of revolutionary martyrs.

Space 5 ft.; **Reach** 5 ft. (10 ft. with ranseur)
Special Attacks force bolt, improved grab
Spell-Like Abilities (CL 8th)
At will—*detect magic, floating disk, mage armor, resist energy, unseen servant*
3/day—*dispel magic, displacement, suggestion* (DC 18)
1/day—*dimension door, resilient sphere* (DC 19)

TACTICS

Before Combat A witchwyrd casts *mage armor* and *displacement* on itself if combat is imminent.
During Combat Witchwyrds prefer to rely on their guards for defense, supplementing their attacks with its own force bolts.
Morale If a battle goes poorly, a witchwyrd casts *resilient sphere*, hoping to catch as many of its foes as possible within the sphere. A witchwyrd reduced to 15 hit points or less flees with the use of *dimension door.*

STATISTICS

Str 16, **Dex** 14, **Con** 14, **Int** 18, **Wis** 13, **Cha** 20
Base Atk +8; **Grp** +15
Feats Deflect Arrows[B], Great Fortitude, Iron Will, Multiattack, Negotiator
Skills Appraise +10, Bluff +16, Concentration +7, Diplomacy +20, Gather Information +10, Knowledge (arcana) +9, Knowledge (geography) +9, Knowledge (the planes) +9, Sense Motive +7, Spot +8
Languages Common, Cyrunian, Draconic, one or more elemental or planar languages; *tongues*

ECOLOGY

Environment any
Organization solitary, entourage (1 witchwyrd and 2–4 human guards), or enclave (3–6 witchwyrds and 11–20 human guards)
Treasure double standard
Advancement by class; **Favored Class** sorcerer
Level Adjustment +7

SPECIAL ABILITIES

Absorb Force (Su) As long as it has at least one hand free, a witchwyrd can "catch" *magic missiles* fired at it. The witchwyrd absorbs the energy from the spell, which manifests as a glowing nimbus around the hand that caught it (which is no longer considered free). The energy can then be used to augment the creature's force bolt ability, adding an additional *magic missile* for each absorbed missile. Absorbed missiles last for 6 rounds before dispersing. A witchwyrd can catch one *magic missile* per free hand per round, and must be aware of the attack and not flat-footed.

Force Bolt (Su) A witchwyrd can "throw" a *magic missile* from each free upper hand as a free action (maximum two per round). These missiles are identical to those created by the *magic missile* spell. The number of missiles thrown can be increased by energy harvested by a witchwyrd's absorb force ability.

Improved Grab (Ex) To use this ability, a witchwyrd must have

WITCHWYRD

This strange figure is draped in flowing robes with a high collar and tall conical hat, bedecked with various pouches, purses, and strange amulets and fetishes. Gray-skinned and just taller than a man, it is generally humanoid in form, with the exception of its four weaving arms, each of which ends in a broad, three-fingered hand. Its luminous yellow eyes suggest an alien intelligence.

WITCHWYRD   **CR 6**

Usually LN Medium monstrous humanoid
Init +2; **Senses** darkvision 60 ft.; **Listen** +1, **Spot** +7

DEFENSE

AC 20, touch 12, flat-footed 18
  (+4 armor, +2 Dex, +4 natural)
hp 52 (8d8+16)
Fort +4, **Ref** +8, **Will** +9
Defensive Abilities absorb force; **DR** 5/magic

OFFENSE

Spd 30 ft.
Melee masterwork ranseur +12 (2d4+4/×3) and
  2 slams +9 (1d4+1) or
  4 slams +11 (1d4+3)

at least two hands free and must hit a Medium or smaller opponent with a slam attack. It can then attempt to start a grapple as a free action without provoking an attack of opportunity. Witchwyrds receive a +4 racial bonus on grapple checks, which is already included in the statistics block.

Tongues (Sp) A witchwyrd can speak with any creature that has a language, as if using a *tongues* spell. This ability is always active.

Witchwyrds ply the hidden paths between planets and planes, traveling and haggling in lands widely believed to be mere legends. Avid wanderers and inveterate merchants, these opportunistic travellers can be found on nearly any world or plane with civilized trade, often with an entourage of strange but loyal bodyguards.

Witchwyrds are humanoid, though with four arms and hairless gray-blue skin. Their uniquely flexible limbs allow them to hide their second pair against the small of their backs with ease, and those who clothe themselves in concealing garb can easily pass for normal, if tall, humanoids. Otherwise, they favor loose, flowing robes in reds and yellows and wear distinctive conical hats. Their eyes glow visibly, increasing in brightness as they absorb force energy. Witchwyrds average 6 1/2 feet in height and weigh up to 300 pounds. Their average lifespan is unknown.

While female witchwyrds do exist, it can be difficult to identify them as such at first glance. Females are slightly shorter and stouter than males, their features tend to be more angular, and their eyes have a greenish glow. Juvenile witchwyrds are also sometimes encountered, almost always as apprentices of established witchwyrd traders, and appear as smaller, softer-skinned versions of their adult kin.

ECOLOGY

Witchwyrds prefer the deserts and tropical climes of the lands they visit, but they might be found anywhere trade is conducted. They eat, sleep, breathe, and bleed like any normal creature, though they also seem to gain some manner of sustenance from the magical force energy they absorb. In regards to more mundane provisions, witchwyrds share a fondness for very spicy foods that would burn the tongues of most humanoids.

HABITAT & SOCIETY

Most witchwyrds encountered are solitary traders, though some band together in small commercial enclaves in areas where trade thrives. Some who engage in regular trade with witchwyrds deduce that, in many if not all cases, a mysterious mercantile oligarchy of witchwyrd elders directs their race's interplanar trade. Individual witchwyrd traders usually claim to be in business only for themselves, however.

Witchwyrds often travel with an entourage of mercenaries hired from among the locals they're dealing with or more exotic creatures from areas they've visited

in the past. These bodyguards tend to be fanatically loyal, even without the use of compulsion magic. Those who serve witchwyrds never speak of what they're being paid or what they've been promised, purportedly forbidden from doing so by highly lucrative contracts.

Each witchwyrd focuses primarily on one area of trade. For example, one witchwyrd might specialize in magic items, another in drugs and narcotics, and still another in Fourth Dynasty Tymarian beetle sculptures. While these individuals might deal in other goods (particularly if one witchwyrd is an area's sole trade representative), their greatest expertise and selection of wares draws from their chosen specialty.

If witchwyrds have one unifying trait, it is their love for haggling. It sometimes seems that the process of bargaining for goods is more important to a witchwyrd than the eventual deal that is struck. They love dickering so much, in fact, that they sometimes undersell their own products just to engage a potential buyer who is uninterested in haggling.

While individual witchwyrds frequently travel across worlds using portals and other known means, rumors tell of a great trading fleet of strange witchwyrd ships capable of sailing across earth and the planes as easily as water.

KNOWN WITCHWYRD MERCHANTS

Witchwyrds are no strangers to the lands of Golarion, with some even having settled there.

Akhenakh: A fixture of the Nightstalls of Katapesh, the witchwyrd Akhenakh's stock in trade is cursed magic. Either buying or selling, he has been known to barter perfectly good magic items for particularly rare or exotic cursed items brought out of lost dungeons by adventurers. Rumors persist that he regularly crates the most potent of his purchases and ships them elsewhere, potentially to some other storehouse or agent.

Cythrul: The female witchwyrd Cythrul runs a shop in the trading city of Hajoth Hakados, where she deals, unsurprisingly, in Numerian skymetal. She does brisk trade selling weapons to pilgrims on their way to the Mendevian Crusades and cultivates good relations with the Technic League, having even gifted them with many strange plans and diagrams.

Grekopek: Based in Bloodcove, the explorer Grekopek is a respected dealer of Mwangi artifacts. He commonly hires independent adventurers to accompany his expeditions into the Mwangi Expanse to recover relics from the ancient ruins of Usaro, Osibu, and Mzali. It is said that he has even visited the fabled Ruins of Kho, but was uninterested in the otherworldly "souvenirs" he found there. Grekopek hides his alien nature, disguising his arms and dressing in the heavy k'sas of the ancient Mwangi.

SAJAN

MALE HUMAN MONK 4
ALIGN LN   INIT +3   SPEED 40 ft.

DEITY: Irori
HOMELAND: Vudra

ABILITIES
13	STR
16	DEX
14	CON
10	INT
12	WIS
8	CHA

DEFENSE
HP 29

AC 16
touch 15, flat-footed 13

Fort +6, Ref +7, Will +5
(+2 against enchantment)

Special Defenses evasion, slow fall 20 ft., still mind

OFFENSE
Melee unarmed strike +4 (1d8+1) or flurry of blows +2/+2 (1d6+1) or temple sword +5 (1d8+1/19–20)
Base Atk +3; **Grp** +4
Special Attacks ki strike (magic), stunning fist 4/day (DC 13)

SKILLS
Climb	+8
Escape Artist	+10
Jump	+14
Sense Motive	+8
Tumble	+12

FEATS
Deflect Arrows, Dodge, Exotic Weapon Proficiency (temple sword), Mobility, Stunning Fist

Combat Gear potion of cure light wounds; **Other Gear** masterwork temple sword, *bracers of armor +1, ring of protection +1*, wooden holy symbol, belt pouch

Sajan Gadadvara and his twin sister Sajni were separated when the lord they served was shamed and forced to cede half his army to the victor—among them Sajan's sister. Sajni was taken away from Vudra by her new master, and Sajan abandoned his own responsibilities to follow. He spent years trying in vain to find her, but has not yet given up. Sajan knows he cannot return to Vudra, for the padapranja there would execute him as a deserter. He cares not for his home country, however, and continues to seek out any clue that might point him toward his sister.

LINI

FEMALE GNOME DRUID 4
ALIGN N   INIT +1   SPEED 20 ft.

DEITY: Green Faith
HOMELAND: Land of the Linnorm Kings

ABILITIES
6	STR
12	DEX
16	CON
10	INT
16	WIS
13	CHA

DEFENSE
HP 33

AC 16
touch 13, flat-footed 15 (+4 bonus against giants)

Fort +7, Ref +2, Will +7
(+2 against illusions)

Special Qualities low-light vision, nature sense, woodland stride

OFFENSE
Melee sickle +2 (1d4–2)
Ranged mwk sling +6 (1d3–2)
Base Atk +3; **Grp** –3
Special Attacks +1 on attack rolls against goblins and kobolds
Spell-Like Abilites (CL 1st)
1/day—*dancing lights, ghost sound* (DC 11), *prestidigitation, speak with burrowing mammals*
Spells Prepared (CL 4th; +5 ranged)
2nd—*barkskin, flame blade, lesser restoration*
1st—*charm animal* (DC 14), *entangle* (DC 14), *longstrider, produce flame*
0—*create water, cure minor wounds, guidance, light, mending*

SKILLS
Concentration	+10
Craft (alchemy)	+2
Handle Animal	+8
Knowledge (nature)	+9
Listen	+5
Ride	+8
Survival	+5
Wild Empathy	+5

FEATS
Augment Summoning, Spell Focus (conjuration)

ANIMAL COMPANION
Droogami (snow leopard; MM 274)

Combat Gear scroll of cure light wounds (2); **Other Gear** *+1 leather armor*, sickle, masterwork sling with 10 bullets, *ring of protection +1*, belt pouch, mistletoe, spell component pouch, sunrods (2), rations (2 days), collection of special de-barked sticks, 5 gp

Lini always seemed to possess a certain affinity with various creatures of the woodlands near where she grew up—particularly with larger predators like bears and snow leopards. More than once, Lini's enclave came under threat from some great bear or razor-clawed cat, but with a series of soothing noises and precise motions she always soothed the beast and sent it on its way. In the years since her departure from the Lands of the Linnorm Kings, Lini has collected more than a dozen sticks—one from each forest or wood she visits. These sticks are to Lini a roadmap of her experiences, and while they may look indistinguishable to others, each holds a wealth of memories to the gnome druid.

SELTYIEL

MALE HALF-ELF
FIGHTER 1/EVOKER 3
ALIGN LE   INIT +2   SPEED 30 ft.
DEITY: Asmodeus
HOMELAND: Cheliax

ABILITIES
12	STR
15	DEX
14	CON
14	INT
8	WIS
10	CHA

DEFENSE
HP 25

AC 15
touch 12, flat-footed 13

Fort +5, Ref +3, Will +2;
+2 against enchantment;
immune to sleep effects

OFFENSE
Melee +1 longsword +5 (1d8+2/19–20)
Ranged mwk shortbow +5 (1d6/×3)
Base Atk +2; **Grp** +3
Special Qualities low-light vision
Spells Prepared (CL 3rd, +4 ranged touch, 10% spell failure)
2nd—bull's strength, mirror image, scorching ray
1st—enlarge person, burning hands (DC 14), magic missile, shield
0—flare (DC 13), light, mage hand, ray of frost, prestidigitation
Prohibited Schools enchantment, necromancy

SKILLS
Concentration	+5
Craft (alchemy)	+9
Diplomacy	+2
Gather Information	+2
Intimidate	+4
Knowledge (arcana)	+7
Listen	+0
Search	+3
Spellcraft	+7
Spot	+0

FEATS
Combat Expertise, Scribe Scroll, Spell Focus (evocation), Weapon Focus (longsword)

FAMILIAR
Dargenti (bat)

Combat Gear acid, alchemist's fire (2); **Other Gear** +1 leather armor, +1 longsword, dagger, masterwork shortbow with 20 arrows, flask of fine absinthe worth 50 gp, gold holy symbol worth 75 gp, spellbook, 8 gp

Born from a dead mother amid screams and disgrace, Seltyiel grew up surrounded by shame and abuse. Before he came of age, his stepfather attempted to murder him, but after Seltyiel turned the tables, he fled into the wild. Since then, his life has been a cruel series of betrayals and pain. His brief reunion with his true father (a notorious bandit) ended with the half-elf being betrayed and imprisoned. Recently released, Seltyiel longs for revenge against both his fathers for his stolen childhood.

AMIRI

FEMALE HUMAN BARBARIAN 4
ALIGN CN   INIT +1   SPEED 30 ft.
DEITY: Gorum
HOMELAND: Realm of the Mammoth Lords

ABILITIES
16	STR
13	DEX
14	CON
10	INT
12	WIS
8	CHA

DEFENSE
HP 39

AC 15
touch 11, flat-footed 14

Fort +6, Ref +2, Will +2

Special Defenses trap sense +1, uncanny dodge

OFFENSE
Melee Large +1 bastard sword +7 (2d8+4/19–20)
Ranged mwk longbow +6 (1d8/×3)
Base Atk +4; **Grp** +7
Special Attacks rage 2/day
Special Qualities fast movement, illiteracy

BARBARIAN RAGE
HP 47
AC 13, touch 9, flat-footed 12
Fort +8, Ref +2, Will +4
Melee Large +1 bastard sword +9 (2d8+8/19–20)
Str 20, Con 18

RAGING POWER ATTACK
Melee Large +1 bastard sword +5 (2d8+16/19–20)

SKILLS
Climb	+6
Intimidate	+6
Jump	+9
Listen	+8
Spot	+3
Survival	+8

FEATS
Exotic Weapon Proficiency (bastard sword), Power Attack, Weapon Focus (bastard sword)

Gear +1 hide armor, Large +1 bastard sword, masterwork longbow, javelins (2), throwing axe, spiked gauntlet, 20 gp

Amiri never quite fit in to the expected gender roles of her tribe, and when the tribe attempted to send her on a suicide mission, she returned with an enormous trophy—a frost giant's sword. She has since abandoned her people, and has come to value her oversized sword (even though she can only truly wield it properly when her blood rage takes her). She never speaks of the circumstances that forced her to flee her homeland. Some things are better left unsaid.

Next Month in PATHFINDER

THE ARMAGEDDON ECHO
by Jason Bulmahn

Celwynvian, the City of Emerald Rains, has long been forbidden to non-elven trespassers, though tales tell of an ancient evil festering in its ruined heart. With the path of the drow and their deadly magic leading to the depths of the eldritch Mierani Forest, the PCs must join with the city's elven protectors to retake the legendary homeland. Yet, invading Celwynvian reveals more than just drow conspirators, pitting the PCs against a memory of a disastrous past that threatens to consume Golarion once more.

CELWYNVIAN
by Amber Scott

Discover the City of Emerald Rains, once among the most magnificent elven cities in all Golarion but now a ruined resting place for wild monstrosities, covetous dragons, and the remnants of the ancient dead. Learn what terrors await in the fabled city, what splendors long to be reclaimed, and what fabulous treasures still glisten amid the rubble.

THE DROW OF GOLARION
by Jeff Grubb

The drow of Golarion revealed! Learn the ways of these long-forgotten but deadly kin to the elves of the surface world. Explore their sinister society, embrace their ageless hatreds, and take your place among the nobility of the dark elf elite!

AND MORE!

Delve into the deadly past with Set Piece: Elven Ruins, and learn what terrors lurk among the remnants of forgotten splendors! Follow Eando Kline's descent into the Darklands, a deceitful wilderness where even seemingly friendly faces can turn deadly in an instant. And discover what lurks beneath forest boughs with a slew of new menaces in the *Pathfinder* Bestiary!

SUBSCRIBE TO PATHFINDER!

Don't miss out on a single encounter! Head on over to **paizo. com/pathfinder** and set up a subscription today! Have each *Pathfinder*, Pathfinder Chronicles, Pathfinder Companion, and GameMastery product delivered to your door!

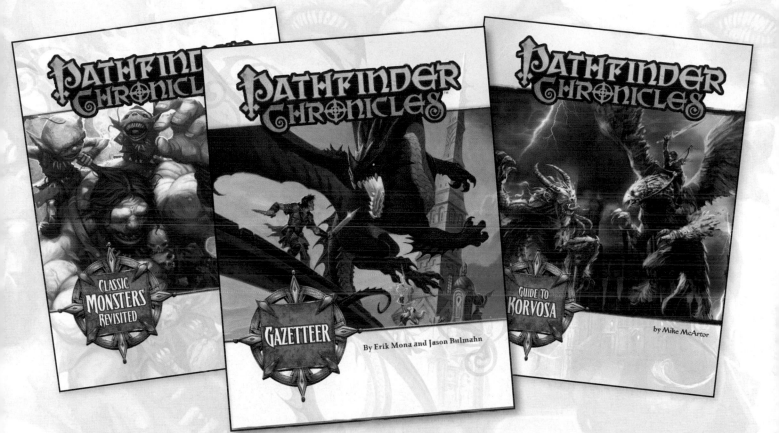

IT'S *YOUR* WORLD NOW.

From the crumbling spires of the ancient runelords in distant Varisia to the bustling merchant kingdoms of the Inner Sea, the *Pathfinder Chronicles* campaign setting forms the panoramic backdrop for Paizo Publishing's innovative *Pathfinder* fantasy roleplaying supplements, modules, and Adventure Paths. The world's most popular roleplaying game is always changing, but the *Pathfinder Chronicles* campaign setting is designed to be great right from the start. Your next great adventure is about to begin. It's *your* world now.

Pathfinder Chronicles Supplements • $17.99

paizo.com/pathfinder
All trademarks are property of Paizo Publishing®,
LLC. ©2008 Paizo. All Rights Reserved

Explore Your World

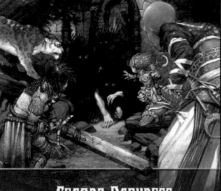

PATHFINDER™

Pathfinder is your monthly *Pathfinder Chronicles* campaign setting Adventure Path source. Each volume explores new locations, unveils new monsters unique to Golarion, and gives Game Masters another entry in a complete campaign. Adventures, wealth, and fame wait within!

Pathfinder #7 Curse of the Crimson Throne: "Edge of Anarchy"	$19.99		❏
Pathfinder #8 Curse of the Crimson Throne: "Seven Days to the Grave"	$19.99		❏
Pathfinder #9 Curse of the Crimson Throne: "Escape from Old Korvosa"	$19.99		❏
Pathfinder #10 Curse of the Crimson Throne: "A History of Ashes"	$19.99		❏
Pathfinder #11 Curse of the Crimson Throne: "Skeletons of Scarwall"	$19.99		❏
Pathfinder #12 Curse of the Crimson Throne: "Crown of Fangs"	$19.99		❏
Pathfinder #13 Second Darkness: "Shadow in the Sky"	$19.99		❏
Pathfinder #14 Second Darkness: "Children of the Void"	$19.99		❏
Pathfinder #15 Second Darkness: "The Armageddon Echo"	$19.99	October, 2008	❏
Pathfinder #16 Second Darkness: "Endless Night"	$19.99	November, 2008	❏
Pathfinder #17 Second Darkness: "A Memory of Darkness"	$19.99	December, 2008	❏
Pathfinder #18 Second Darkness: "Descent into Midnight"	$19.99	January, 2009	❏

PATHFINDER CHRONICLES™

Golarion is the world of Paizo's *Pathfinder Chronicles* campaign setting. Previously only explored via *Pathfinder* and the Pathfinder Modules, these evocative accessories give Game Masters exciting new looks into previously unexplored locales. Don't miss out on a single one—it's *your* world now.

Pathfinder Chronicles: Guide to Korvosa	$17.99		❏
Pathfinder Chronicles: Gazetteer	$17.99		❏
Pathfinder Chronicles: Classic Monsters Revisited	$17.99		❏
Pathfinder Chronicles: Guide to Darkmoon Vale	$17.99		❏
Pathfinder Chronicles: Campaign Setting (Hardcover)	$49.99		❏
Pathfinder Chronicles: Gods & Magic	$17.99	October, 2008	❏
Pathfinder Chronicles: Into the Darklands	$17.99	November, 2008	❏
Pathfinder Chronicles: Guide to Absalom	$17.99	December, 2008	❏
Pathfinder Chronicles: Second Darkness Map Folio	$14.99	January, 2009	❏

PATHFINDER™ COMPANION

Each *Pathfinder Companion* explores a major theme in the *Pathfinder Chronicles* campaign setting, with expanded regional gazetteers, new player character options, and organizational overviews to help players flesh out their character backgrounds and to provide players and Game Masters with new sources for campaign intrigue.

Pathfinder Companion: Second Darkness	$9.99		❏
Pathfinder Companion: Elves of Golarion	$9.99	October, 2008	❏
Pathfinder Companion: Osirion, Land of Pharaohs	$9.99	December, 2008	❏

GAMEMASTERY™

Every good Game Master needs good game accessories and Paizo's GameMastery line has exactly what you need to enhance your Second Darkness Adventure Path experience!

GameMastery Critical Hit Deck	$9.95		❏
GameMastery Critical Fumble Deck	$9.99		❏
GameMastery Combat Pad	$16.95		❏
GameMastery Flip-Mat: Darklands	$12.99		❏
GameMastery Map Pack: Elven City	$12.99	October, 2008	❏
GameMastery Map Pack: Ancient Forest	$12.99	December, 2008	❏

GOLARION NEEDS HEROES

The exciting world of the *Pathfinder*™ Adventure Paths and *Pathfinder* Modules comes alive in this massive 256-page full-color hardcover tome primed and ready to go for your new campaign! Detailed sections on more than 40 nations provide a full picture of the world of the *Pathfinder Chronicles*™ campaign setting, with new rules, new magic and spells, detailed descriptions of more than twenty gods, and a gorgeous poster map detailing the entire campaign setting.

Written by
Keith Baker, Wolfgang Baur, Jason Bulmahn, Ed Greenwood, Jeff Grubb, James Jacobs, Mike McArtor, Erik Mona, F. Wesley Schneider, and more than twenty additional authors, including mini-essays on world creation by R.A. Salvatore and Robert J. Kuntz.

Pathfinder Chronicles Campaign Setting:
Available Now ♦ $49.99

paizo.com/pathfinder